"When I first met Carrielynn, her love for people and her passion for Jesus were unmistakeable. This love and passion have driven her desire to help women around her. Her hope for this book comes with a sincere care for others who have found themselves under the weight of the world. Her longing is to help the broken find their way to Jesus, who offers a living water so that we may be restored. This is Carrielynn's purpose and I have been amazed to see the impact she continues to have on women around her as she leads people to Jesus."

–**Nick Schonlau**
Groups Minister
Third City Christian Church, Grand Island, NE
/ *thirdcityc.org*

"Carrielynn is truly an incredible soul! Her passion and enthusiasm for life and for Jesus are absolutely infectious; I knew within moments of meeting her that God placed her in my life for a reason. While Carrielynn exudes peace and joy in every interaction, her life has not been without trial or pain. But what makes Carrielynn so special is how she's allowed God to *use* those experiences to shape her and to bless others. I speak from experience that you can't walk away from a conversation with Carrielynn without feeling loved and without encountering Jesus. *Unstoppable Peace* is sure to impact your heart and change your perspective!"

–**Brittney Parr**
Global Change Management Lead
Certified Professional Coach

UNSTOPPABLE Peace
A STORY OF FAITH

How God Uses
Forgiveness to Restore
Beauty from Ashes

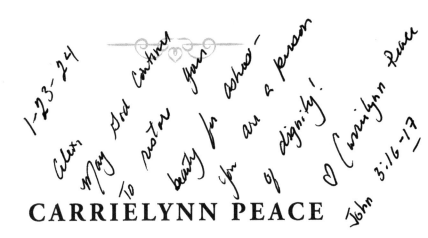

CARRIELYNN PEACE

Copyright 2023 by Carrielynn Peace

Published through Electric Moon Publishing, LLC

©2023 *UNSTOPPABLE PEACE: A Story of Faith – How God Uses Forgiveness to Restore Beauty from Ashes* / Carrielynn Peace

Paperback ISBN-13: 978-1-943027-69-9
E-book ISBN-13: 978-1-943027-70-5

Electric Moon Publishing, LLC
P.O. Box 466
Stromsburg, NE 68666
info@emoonpublishing.com

All rights reserved. No part of this publication may be reproduced, distributed, or transmitted in any form or by any means, including photocopying, recording, or other electronic or mechanical methods, without the prior written permission of the publisher, except in the case of brief quotations embodied in critical reviews and certain other noncommercial uses permitted by copyright law. For permission requests, write to the publisher.

The opinions and quotations of the author are not necessarily those of the publisher or its affiliates. Author retains all intellectual property rights. Contact the author with questions.

All websites listed herein are accurate at the time of publication, but may change in the future or cease to exist. The listing of website references and resources does not imply publisher/author endorsement of the site's entire contents. Groups, corporations, and organizations are listed for informational purposes, and listing does not imply publisher/author endorsement of activities.

Scripture quotations are from the The Holy Bible, English Standard Version® and are marked (ESV), copyright © 2001 by Crossway, a publishing ministry of Good News Publishers. Used by permission. All rights reserved. The ESV text may not be quoted in any publication made available to the public by a Creative Commons license. The ESV may not be translated into any other language.

Scripture quotations marked (NASB) are taken from the New American Standard Bible®, Copyright © 1960, 1971, 1977, 1995, 2020 by The Lockman Foundation. Used by permission. All rights reserved. www.lockman.org

Scripture quotations marked (MSG) are taken from The Message, copyright © 1993, 2002, 2018 by Eugene H. Peterson. Used by permission of NavPress. All rights reserved. Represented by Tyndale House Publishers.

Scripture quotations marked (NIV) are taken from the Holy Bible, New International Version®, NIV®. Copyright © 1973, 1978, 1984, 2011 by Biblica, Inc.™ Used by permission of Zondervan. All rights reserved worldwide. www.zondervan.com The "NIV" and "New International Version" are trademarks registered in the United States Patent and Trademark Office by Biblica, Inc.™

Scripture quotations marked (KJV) are taken from The Authorized (King James) Version. Rights in the Authorized Version in the United Kingdom are vested in the Crown. Reproduced by permission of the Crown's patentee, Cambridge University Press.

Editing by Electric Moon Publishing Editorial Services
Cover and interior design by D.E. West, ZAQ Designs - www.zaqdesigns.com
Electric Moon Publishing Creative Services
www.emoonpublishing.com

Printed in the United States of America

www.emoonpublishing.com

Dedicated to God, the hero of each of our stories,
and to all of those God gave me
to love, lead, encourage, teach, and mentor,
especially my beloved Thomas, Heidi, Rachel,
and my grandchildren.

CONTENTS

Dear Reader ix
Introduction..xi

Chapter 1: Shattered 1
Chapter 2: Trust..9
Chapter 3: Character...23
Chapter 4: Vulnerability..31
Chapter 5: Change 39
Chapter 6: Acceptance...49
Chapter 7: Remembering 55
Chapter 8: Choices..63
Chapter 9: Transformed 81
Chapter 10: Shattered 101
Chapter 11: Reckoning 119
Setting Your Own Goals...129

Addendum 145
Glossary 151

Dear Reader,

The storms that were devised to destroy Faith proved to be an opportunity to rebuild. More than an opportunity, they forced her to rebuild. If you have ever looked out the window of your life after it has been hit by a tornado or some other natural disaster, you know that sense of holding your breath as you see if anything survived. If you recently weathered a storm like that, run to a mirror. Look—you're still here. So this is a good day to start picking up the pieces and get to work.

Faith endured abandonment, humiliation, shame from her own lousy choices, feeling that she was not enough, and so much more. Eventually she learned to grasp the hand of the one who knew her best as He ran to her rescue.

This book is the result of a promise I made to God, to comfort those with the same comfort He so beautifully and completely provided to me. He was my person; the one I could lean on when the walls of my life collapsed. As with Faith's life, the rubble tried to suggest that *this mess was beyond repair*. That was a lie. But it was a big mess.

My life was hit by a category-five storm. But the Rescuer had seen devastation like this before. He knew how to reconstruct the ruins. So I took His hand and we started to move the debris of my shattered life. I set emotional, spiritual, financial, educational, physical, and social goals. God helped me to reconstruct my life. I lost one hundred pounds, ran a marathon at forty-nine years old, earned a master's degree after I became a grandma, and most importantly, found an enriching community with whom to live and to do ministry. In this book I will share that process.

The answers to my many whelps for help were found during the thousands of hours in which I cried out to Him with my Bible open and my pen etching every truth He taught me into my well-worn journal. So within each chapter we will open our Bibles together and engrave the truths we learn onto a page and into our hearts; that is where I found healing. I pray that the story of Faith is the inspiration you need to write your own story of *Unstoppable Peace*.

With love,
Carrielynn

INTRODUCTION

*So do not fear, for I am with you do; not be dismayed,
for I am your God. I will strengthen you and help you;
I will uphold you with my righteous right hand.*
(Isaiah 41:10 NIV)

Haven't I already lost enough?

After finally allowing herself to love someone, Faith would learn that love and trust are not always guaranteed, no matter how hard she tried. How would she care for her children? Had her sacrifices all been a waste? If she offered forgiveness, was she playing the fool? Who could understand her heartbreak? God proved that He was watching every step she took and that He had a plan, even when all seemed destroyed. God was never late.

My friend, Faith is a composite character who is based on true stories of women I have walked beside as well as my own life. Most importantly, her story explains how God led all of us through some heart-wrenching days and how we participated with Him to change everything. Dear reader, He will do the same for you.

During the thousands of hours I spent studying His ways, His life, and His desires for my healing, He taught me to see myself differently. At the end of this book we will discuss goals for your life, just in case you believe God is calling you to trust Him for something better. Because I believe that for you!

I want you to imagine that you are sitting across the table

from your best friend—the friend you can tell everything to who is cheering for your success. That is me. If you have never had a friend like that, you do now. I am going to tell you about how I conquered my fears and how God changed everything in my life. I will share my "aha" moments and the tears that were replaced by confidence as I worked toward facing the chaos I lived in and replaced it with a peaceful life.

Who I am today, by God's grace, is not who I was. Over the years I have lost 100 pounds, finalizing that huge endeavor during my darkest days. I have run a marathon and earned my master's degree. Most importantly, I am at peace with who I am and with my life.

Life forced me to accomplish these things. I had to take care of myself and rebuild my life so my grown kids would not worry about me. That led to putting every aspect of my life in God's hands and gripping His hand as though it was all I had. Because it was. He was and is my strength.

It really was. All. I. Had.

I know this book is being picked up by some precious friends I have known for years and some who are just beginning to be new friends. Welcome to all. My new friends, I can't wait for us to get to know each other. We will laugh. We will cry. We will dream. We will be honest about our failures, and we will love. We will love each other's successes and dream each other's dreams. My old friends, thank you for the love and support, especially on my toughest days. It was shocking for you, I know, as my wrecked life poured out like a gushing river that riverbanks or levees couldn't hold in.

I will explain not just what needed to happen in my life but also the why and the how. I will also tell you great and hilarious stories of the whos—who helped and who I needed to stay away from, because one of the significant lessons I learned was that boundaries are biblical.

Last, I don't want you to get to a great place in your career, health, or finances only to have it stripped away by not being warned about the little devils that want to steal your successes from you. They are out there. Believe me. As you change your own life, there will be those who are trying to pull you back into the ugly life that you are trying to crawl out of.

Bad characters will threaten your success; they hate to see you move into your purpose and into a life of beauty and dignity. Why do I think you should be aware of this? Because part of what kept me on track was seeing women who had gone before me who fell into the snares and never recovered or were terminally set back. I do not want that for you.

I also want to tell you what I needed to be told—what I needed to hear time and time again. I needed to know the value of my own life and dreams. That came only with knowing God better and believing what He said about my life.

It was not easy, but it was great. Really great. I want your life to be boundless and to be all that God has planned for you.

Chapter 1
Shattered

"When did things go off the rails?" The church counselor's stinging probe had immersed Faith in quicksand. Clawing to search the dark tunnel of her pain, she grappled through the roots and pestilence for a glimmer. She searched her mind for when the path had been clear. It seemed like a lifetime ago.

As intense as the morning sun glaring through her shades, she remembered the day her life derailed, although it felt as if she and Robert had lived two lives, one when they were happy and their current one. In reality, it had been one life—a life of choices she'd piled on each other like a mountain of decayed bones.

Exhausted, Faith hobbled over to the elevator. A heavy sigh lifted from her chest as she nudged the button to take her up to her room. Stomping the ruby-red stilettos that she had forced herself to wear, knowing Robert liked them, it hit Faith that the key to her room was in her purse. "Oh, brother." She rolled her eyes, turning on her heel, remembering both were under the table where she had been sitting. Stomping toward the shiny, ingrained wood floor, reentering the extravagant room, she pasted on a smile and succumbed to a glide to retrieve her things.

As she took each high step, she could feel a thud in her eyes and the front of her head, resembling a sledgehammer. She winced as she looked for the table. Her pupils tried to adjust to the dark room. The shadows at the table came into focus, and her heart shattered like chards from a window that had been struck with a sniper's shot.

The dream she and Robert had built years ago would never be the same.

The Dream

Running a brush through her long, golden strands, using both hands to capture it all and tie it with a thick band, Faith would have loved to spend a little more time playing in front of the mirror that morning, but Saturdays, just like the rest of the week, had a list of responsibilities a mile long. Today didn't look as if it would be any different.

Taking in a full view of how her hair, tucked-in blouse, and snug jeans looked from the back, she was satisfied. She shrugged, thinking it was as good as it was going to get. *Who cares anyway? It's just work.*

The eight-mile jaunt from the next town over was nothing to him. Robert's dad had pushed him into this job since Mr. Ryan knew the manager of the store and knew he'd kindle the work ethic for which the Ryan family was notorious. Now Robert was glad he did. He recalled the ribbing he took the evening before after their team's win.

"Why do you do that to yourself, man?" The leading lineman shook his head. "Working Saturdays?"

"I have reasons. My job will make a way for my future." Robert yanked the door to his ten-year-old car open.

"Man, you sound like my dad." The kicker shook his head and climbed into his new black Chevy truck.

"I know." Robert grinned and climbed into his dilapidated Celica. It wasn't worth his breath to go into it. He came from an upper-middle-class family, like them, and while they had jobs too, they were still in bed while he was at work on Saturday morning.

Robert was a leader on the field—a straight-A student and had a part-time job; always striving toward his next goal helped him become a great team captain. He set the pace wherever he landed.

Robert felt his heart beating through his crisp white shirt; it boomed like the snare drum that pounded at his game the night before as he scored another touchdown. Quickly spinning into the parking spot, he couldn't leap out of his car fast enough.

"Faith, hey, Faith!" he called out a little louder. "Wait up!"

"Hi, Robert." Faith's soft voice seemed to sing as she grinned. As she stretched her neck toward the clouds to greet him, he thought he saw her deep blue eyes sparkle. Her hair bounced as she trotted in, trying to make it on time. "I didn't know you worked today," she said as he caught up to her.

Robert reminded himself to calm his toothy smile. "Yeah, I asked to be put on the schedule every Saturday."

"Cool. Me too," Faith said, telling Robert something he already knew.

Faith liked working with Robert. He made the days go by faster; he was a nice guy and worked hard. She had no idea that Robert had requested the Saturday morning shift because of her.

"Do you have any plans after work tonight?" Robert asked, streaking his sweaty palms down his pants as he caught his breath.

"I'm not sure." Faith's smile broadened as she looked up at him, then dashed toward the door.

Robert's legs still ached from the game the night before. He sprinted to keep up and hopefully get an answer.

They waited at the time clock, taking turns to start their day. Engrossed in his white high tops and grateful that they gave him somewhere to ponder his next words, he glanced at Faith, brushed his long bangs to the side of his otherwise clean-cut head, and smiled. "I, uhm, wondered if maybe we could grab something to eat?" *Man, I sound like an idiot. Did my voice really just squeak like a seventh-grader? Well, there goes my chance. Kiss this idea goodbye.*

"That sounds like fun." Faith interrupted Robert's spiraling thoughts. Her tiny, freckled cheeks framed her dimpled smile.

Like a tidal wave hitting the sand, her grin washed away his fears.

She strolled toward her manager. "I'll give my dad a call later and see whose turn it is to cook dinner, but I'll let you know what he says before you head out to eat."

Robert wondered if Faith thought this was just one friend inviting another one to hang out. He had practiced asking her out for the last couple of weeks, and he had expected it to go more smoothly than this.

"Hey, Robert. Sorry, but my dad asked me to come home tonight to help him manage baths with my sisters and help my brother with homework. Maybe another time?"

His heart sunk beneath his apron. "Sounds good." This was not going as planned.

Nothing came easy for Robert. He woke before dawn every day to be at the field, where he ran and did push-ups before practice even started. Late into the evening, his books were open. His light went off hours after the rest of the family was in bed. Earning As in French and business had taken their toll on his sleep. But he chided himself as he crawled beneath his covers. *Dreams don't just happen—they are earned.*

Faith had dreams of her own. Hers were simple: a peaceful life with two kids, a white picket fence in a little house, and a husband who would be around forever.

Unstoppable Truth: Shattered

In this section we will study the book of Esther. That is where I found peace as each morning before the sun greeted the day, I sat with this Old Testament parchment. I asked God for direction and wisdom during my own shattered moments. Esther offered me insight into God's providential plans; even when we are not looking for Him, He reveals Himself. Faith will lean on these truths as well.

Robert was well known because he was a successful athlete and a good student. His accomplishments opened doors for him. We've all known people like him; maybe you are one. Popularity doesn't eliminate the need we all have to be known and cared about by others. It does not necessarily mean it will lead to a romantic relationship, but being connected is a healthy human need.

What Robert did was scary; he put himself out there. That took courage.

Can you remember the last time you took a chance, putting yourself out there? What were the circumstances? How did it turn out? Life is about seizing opportunity. What opportunities, whether personally or professionally, have pushed you out of your comfort zone?

In the past, have you ever known you were being called to take a risk? Did you do it? If not, do you have any regrets? What are they?

What changes do you need to take? What is next for you?

Please read Esther 1:1–2:8. While this is lengthy, it is so helpful to see God's providential hand in our lives—lives that require courageous decisions.

In this chapter from Esther, what acts of courage do you see?

This section is hard to swallow. I like things to be fair and clear. No, reframe that . . . I need things to be fair! Because of this drunken leader and his rotten comrades, it doesn't seem fair, does it? Have you ever seen God show up when life seems unfair?

Reflection: Can God use people's crummy choices to bring about His plan? When have you seen Him do that?

Dear God,

Please be with us today. Sometimes it is a scary place down here, and many of us have learned that courage can be difficult, and sometimes, just downright unsafe. Please, Lord, help us to step out of our comfort zone.

God, maybe I need to begin to be more courageous with You, to trust You more. Please help me. I vow to You that I will take the following action by the date listed below.

Action: _____

Date: _____

Signed: _____

Chapter 2

Trust

It didn't matter how many times she weaved down the long driveway; during each trek she made toward the old house, she felt a gulf of emptiness wash over her. Taking a deep breath, she put on a smile and walked through the back door to the farmhouse, as she had done for years. The family was sitting around the table, ready to eat dinner. Faith scooted herself between her dad and two-year-old Elizabeth, the baby of the family. Bending over, she kissed Baby Betty, a nickname she gave her when she was born.

Betty reached for her with a big smile, showing all eight of her tiny, square, chiclet teeth. Faith's father, Mr. George, gently patted Betty's small back and shook his head as he sat up from his slump. He widened his red eyes as if trying to wake himself up while he lifted the pan of roast beef and vegetables, putting some on each child's plate. Faith slid the dishes toward each of her five siblings. The system they developed almost two years ago was seamless. Dad dished; Faith assisted. It was the way it had to be now.

After the younger kids had their fill of food, they cleared the table while Faith's dad tried to catch up with his oldest child. "Hon, how was work?" His quiet tone and the curve in his back alerted Faith that he had exhausted himself on the farm that day.

"It was Okay." Faith placed the plates in the large sink, then rubbed her eyes with the back of her wet hand.

Mr. George pushed in each dark, oak dining chair. "Who's that young man I saw stocking shelves at the store the other day?" A well-known businessman as well as a farmer, her father was doing his best at small talk.

"Oh, that's Robert. He goes to St. Francis," Faith said. "That's who asked if I could grab something to eat tonight."

"Looks like he's a hard worker."

Faith wrapped up the last piece of roast and headed toward the refrigerator. A smile spread across her face, connecting the freckles on her cheeks. "Yeah, we like to work together. We race to see who can get our shelves done faster. I won today." Turning back toward her dad, she flexed her arms as if she were Popeye, as her grin broadened.

"That's good." He nodded his approval, then parsed out nuggets of praise to the kids based on their work ethic or academic success. Faith gave him credit for the effort. She knew her father was trying to do it all. He was still adapting to being a single parent. She wondered if Baby Betty was the hardest for him to care for, but he cherished and doted over her. She was Dad's last gift from Mom.

Faith's mind wandered back to the grocery store, pondering why Robert seemed preoccupied. *It wasn't hard to outwork him today.*

The next Saturday, as Faith pulled into her usual parking spot, she noticed Robert was in his car next to the space where she always parked. As he combed his hair, she saw him jolt his mirror back into place as she parked. *Weird! He's only going to stock shelves. Whatever.*

"Hi, Faith." He practically jumped out of his car. Robert had looked forward to seeing her all week. And she did not let him down. She smiled at him, and he returned the gesture with an expression he tried to contain. Though he was thrilled to see her, he managed his emotions, trying to look aloof, as his jock friends did with girls.

The night before, even though he had been shoved and tackled, his team eventually lifted him in the air at the end of the game. Victories on the field wore him out, but he was not too tired for the high point of his week, seeing Faith.

"Happy Saturday, Robert." Her greeting sounded like a song. Her white blouse, blonde hair, and bubbly persona were more refreshing than the glow in the sky. "How was your week?"

"Well, school was good, but our game last night was epic." He paused, prepared to share the reel highlights he had rehearsed in his mind.

"That's awesome," she said, interrupting his announcement. "Race?" She reached up, tapped his shoulder, and sprinted off.

Robert's long stride could have outdone her, but this morning he settled for a jog, which was enough to keep up.

She glanced over her shoulder at him, smiling. Between breaths he got his question out. "Faith, I was wondering if it was your turn to cook tonight." He remembered his heartbreak from the week before.

"Nope, it's my dad's. He was putting dinner in the Crock-Pot when I left."

Robert's heart raced. "Do you want to grab dinner after our shift?"

"Sure, why not?" She shrugged her petite shoulders. "But I might get off before you. I work faster than you, but I'll wait." She flashed a smile and flipped her long hair over her shoulder. "Just don't take too long."

She is gorgeous. Robert's thoughts caught him off guard. He had to gather himself. "We'll see about that. I'll take it easy on you today." Striding beside her, he looked her in the eye.

Faith noticed for the first time—his long eyelashes framing his glittering blue eyes. She sped up and jetted toward the front door, reminding him that the competition was still on.

Robert's long legs outran her, but both were stopped at the automatic door that seemed way too slow this morning.

After work, Robert and Faith strolled out to their cars together. Faith had called her dad and asked if she could go to dinner with Robert.

"I guess that would be Okay." Her dad hesitated, sounding different than when Faith had asked about going out to dinner with other friends.

Oh, well—we're just friends.

"Robert, I feel gross after working all day. Do you mind following me to my house before we go to dinner? I want to get cleaned up."

"No problem," Robert answered, grateful to spend time with her other than at work.

As Robert followed Faith out of town and toward the country, he realized he had never ventured through the deserted roads this far out. Looking down at his gas gauge, he was grateful his dad was meticulous about keeping the tank above half full. Other than her being the friendliest and prettiest girl ever, he realized he didn't know much about Faith, which made him glad she was giving him a chance. *Man, I'm the luckiest dude in the world.*

Gravel kicked up from the road that was lined with corn stalks towering six feet over the top of his car. Robert did his best to keep up with Faith as she maneuvered the curves of the road like a race car driver. Pulling up just behind her, he followed her lead and came to an abrupt stop near a three-story red barn and a white farmhouse that looked like something Robert had seen in an old Western movie. Faith stuck her hand out the window and motioned for him to park next to her Town and Country, complete with the wood panel, the relic she drove, which her dad tried to persuade her was a classic. She couldn't be convinced.

As Robert opened his car door, a man tall enough to block the sun exited the barn. Dressed in a suit and tie but with old dirty cowboy boots on, Robert thought this intimidating figure looked out of place with an old bucket in his hand.

"Hi, sweetie." He leaned way down to kiss Faith on the forehead, keeping his eyes on Robert.

"Hi, Dad." Faith leaned into her father's kiss.

Robert's cheeks flushed red, feeling as if he didn't belong as he watched the warmth between them.

"This is my friend Robert. I told you about him. We work together, and we're going to go grab some dinner."

"Hello, sir." Robert pulled his shoulders back, making his chest expand as he reached his hand out.

"Hi, Robert." Faith's dad dropped the metal bucket and met his grip with a firm shake.

Remembering this kid from the grocery store, Faith's father began to size him up. His spunky, attractive, adventurous daughter had always had male friends, but was this more? Faith sure didn't seem giddy or overly excited. "Where are you kids heading?" Faith's dad squinted in the sunshine, glancing at Faith, then at Robert.

"I don't know," Faith admitted. "First I need to take a shower. I thought I'd introduce Robert to the kids."

"Robert, did Faith inform you that she has five ornery siblings?" Mr. George asked, shaking his head.

"I think she mentioned it."

"Did she mention that they are like a pack of wild wolves?" Faith's dad cupped his massive hand over his ruddy cheeks and rubbed his chin. He lifted his eyebrows toward Faith as if to say, *Did you warn this poor guy?*

"Dad, they're fine."

Robert shifted back and forth as a chuckle slipped out.

"Come on in, Robert. My awesome brother and adorable sisters will *entertain*—you while I take a quick shower." Faith sneered playfully at her dad.

"Entertain, now that's a good word for it." Faith's dad cleared his throat and grabbed his bucket, ambling back toward the barn.

The earsplitting squeak of the back door announced their arrival as they entered the orange and olive linoleum-decorated kitchen. Glasses and bowls filled the sink. Robert heard what he thought sounded like a herd of cattle running on hardwood floors. Faith entered first, with Robert standing about a foot over Faith's head. The stampede stopped in its tracks.

Looking up at Robert were four little Faiths. They had pigtails, blue eyes, and smiles like their big sis. One lanky kid who looked like the man Robert had just met appeared as well. He was maybe thirty years younger.

"What's up, guys?" Faith asked.

"Nothing," ten-year-old Mary answered. She narrowed her eyes at Robert, sizing him up.

"Nutting," said Betty, already in her jammies, smiling back and forth at Faith and Robert.

Raising her arms, Faith scooped her up and placed the toddler on her hip.

"Who's he?" Johnny, Faith's twelve-year-old brother, got right to the point.

"Hey, everyone—this is my friend from work, Robert." Faith nodded and smiled at Robert, noticing that he had been rubbing the side of his pockets with both hands since he entered the house.

"Hey." Robert stumbled over his tongue, and five sets of glaring eyes proved that he was facing a jury.

"Will you guys hang with him while I go take a shower?"

"You know how to throw a football?" Faith's brother, Johnny, asked. His tone seemed to carry a lot of expectation and some doubt.

"Coach calls me Gunslinger if that means anything," Robert boasted, grateful for the distraction.

"I'd like to see it," Faith's kid brother challenged.

Robert appreciated the effort the kid made to put on some middle school confidence.

"While you two throw the ball around, I am going to jump in the shower," Faith announced.

Before Robert could say *punt*, they were out in the open pasture. Robert thought he had better go easy on Faith's little brother. Just as Robert was wondering what this youngster could do, Johnny pulled back his arm and yelled to Robert to go long. The ball sailed through the air like a rocket.

Robert could not believe the power that emerged from this scrawny boy. *At least his arm matches his cockiness.*

As they were getting to know one another, earning each other's respect, the little girls, Mary, Margo, Victoria, and Betty, scurried into the garden near them and planted themselves there, snagging tiny wild strawberries.

Robert snapped the ball, and this time he yelled, "Run hard!" He wielded all the power he had left and launched the pass into the air. As the sphere soared toward the blinding sun, all of a sudden it was picked off by Faith's dad.

Mr. George nodded toward Johnny. "Okay, little Boomer, it's time for supper."

As Johnny raced ahead of them both, Mr. George got in step with Robert and whispered, "I haven't seen Johnny this happy in a long time. Since . . ." The void of words hung in space like the bright ball over the fields. "Thank you."

Surprised by the compliment, Robert was also puzzled, wishing Mr. George had finished his thought, but he knew not to ask. "It was fun for me too. That was a great catch, sir!" Robert was genuinely impressed and didn't hide it.

"Thanks. Been doing a bit more of that lately between farming and going to the office." Mr. George shrugged.

As Robert and Mr. George were nearing the house, Faith came to the door with her hair pulled into a ponytail and a daffodil-colored ribbon dangling from it. Wearing jean shorts, a frilly yellow top, and Dr. Martens, she looked as if she could be on the front of a magazine.

Robert gawked. *This girl is a perfect combination of gorgeous and sporty.*

"Ready?" She leaped from the porch, not touching the three steps. "Daddy, I'll be back after dinner."

"Have fun, kids," Mr. George said. "Nice to meet you," he added, putting his bear-like grip out.

"Thank you, sir," Robert fumbled, then gripped his hand.

As they stepped toward the car, Robert glanced at Faith. *How am I here? With this girl?* Rushing to the passenger side, he grabbed the handle before she could. With his arm crossing his waist and a slight bow for effect, he opened the door and flashed a sincere look of joy as Faith caught his eye.

Amused, she returned his expression. "Thanks, but I can open my own door." Putting one long, tan leg into the car and then the other, she made herself comfortable.

Robert hoped this was to be the first of many times he would have the chance to open her door.

Just as they were about to pull away, Robert glanced into his rearview mirror. Johnny was a mannequin, watching from the porch. Gliding his stick shift back into park, Robert opened his door and stood, calling toward the house, "Hey, Johnny—thanks for giving me a workout! You have a great arm, man!" Johnny waved. As his lips turned upward, he wiped his feet on the weathered mat, then stepped inside.

Faith beamed.

As the car twisted through the gravel drive, the options for dinner filled the awkward spaces in the car. There was a little food truck nearby known for its great burritos, but there was nowhere to sit. Robert hoped to get to know Faith, so this didn't seem like the best choice for a first date. *Is this a date?* Robert silently quizzed himself. There was also the tiny grocery store with a deli and a few tables where they could sit. "How about the diner in the grocery store?" Robert asked, mentioning they could sit there.

Everyone knew Faith's family there, and Faith knew that would open the door to interrogations about Faith's guy friend. Out of the question. "No, let's keep looking." Faith looked over her left shoulder, smiling.

Chatter and laughter filled the car. Robert told Faith about her little brother's amazing passes and her dad's astonishing catch. She told Robert that the little girls prattled on about him when they came in to wash up for dinner.

Faith replayed the conversation in her mind.

"He's a football star. Did you see his arm?" Victoria, though five years old, sounded like a coach.

"Yeah," said Margo, Faith's mini-me and self-appointed spy for the day. "He and Johnny are having a blast." A smile spread across her face as she reported the happenings going on outside, nodding at four-year-old Victoria, wearing a strawberry-stained shirt.

"Johnny really likes him. I can tell." Mary's face lit up. "He is having a lot of fun playing football." When Mary spoke, the family tuned in. She kept her words and thoughts to a minimum, especially in the last couple of years. Faith trusted her opinion.

"What do you think?" Faith asked Mary.

"Seems Okay, but we'll see." Mary tucked her heart safely behind a shield.

"What did they say?" Robert interrupted her thoughts.

"Mostly that they like you."

"Mostly?" Robert glanced at Faith's glowing locks and full smile.

"Johnny hasn't smiled like that in forever." Faith shifted her torso to get comfortable and to face Robert as he drove toward town.

Robert didn't ask why her brother didn't smile much. He knew that a house without a mom was the reason. The void was as wide as a football field. Robert would wait until Faith was ready to share what had happened. As he drove, he put his thoughts aside to be present with the most amazing girl he knew.

Unstoppable Truth: Trust

Trust is hard to build. Once earned, it is critical to protect. Faith watched to see if she could trust Robert. First she observed him at work. She saw how he treated other people. He greeted everyone with a smile and said hello. When fellow workers grumbled about their tasks, he would get to work. He was always the first to hold the door for others or help older folks out to their cars with their groceries. Because of those virtues, she wanted to get to know him better.

Please read Esther 2:5–23.

1. Who did Esther learn she could trust in her childhood (Esther 2:7)? What sacrifice had he made?

2. When she was placed in the citadel of Susa, who could Esther rely on (Esther 2:8)? How did he treat her?

3. How did Esther continue to honor Mordecai (Esther 2:10)?

4. How did Mordecai continue to care for Esther (Esther 2:11)? What do you think was running through his mind? What would be running through your mind?

5. Because Esther trusted Hegai, what did she decide when she went before the king?
    - What was the reaction of everyone who saw her (Esther 2:15b)?

- What was the king's reaction?
- What secret did Esther continue to keep?

6. The foundation of trust is built one brick at a time. How did Mordecai show himself to be faithful to King Xerxes, or as other versions refer to him, King Ahasuerus (Esther 2:21–23)?
   - What was the outcome?

Dear friend,

Think about a person you trust. How has he or she proven to be trustworthy? Sadly, for some of us, at different times, the list is short. Remember—there is one Person you can always trust. That is God. He will never leave you, and He will never forsake you. He promises to stick closer than a brother. He has proven this in my life time and time again. As you pray and read His Word, the Bible, you will find Him! I promise!

Be blessed!

Carrielynn

Chapter 3

Character

The days became weeks, and the weeks added up to months. Can true love happen that quickly? Time would tell.

Robert had already fallen hard for Faith. She was different from any other girl he knew.

On an early Saturday morning at the grocery store, Faith howled, "Robert, come quickly!" She was in the produce area while he had been lining cans on the bottom shelf in the next aisle over.

"Just finishing up. Be right there," Robert promised.

"Robert, come now!" Faith squealed.

Robert, running around the corner, dashed to see what had happened. Just as he peeked at her, Faith's arm was outstretched and her long index finger shook toward the produce she had been arranging. "Catch it!" A huge snake sat between two cantaloupes, peeking its head out.

Robert went to grab it, prepared to be the hero when he heard Faith begin to roar with laughter. Clutching it, he shook the authentic-looking rubber snake in Faith's face, twisting the flexible neck back and forth. Taking in a deep breath, he smiled and rolled his eyes. Slinging the pretend anaconda over his shoulder, he planned to put it in the breakroom.

"Put it back. Pleeeeease," she whined.

Robert's smile framed his wide blue eyes. "The store opens in ten minutes."

"I know." Faith snickered, hoping he would want to join in her Saturday antics.

"We better not. It would be bad for business." His smile broadened.

"Imagine if some kid came in and saw it, Robert. It would be hilarious." Faith tried to get him on her side.

"I think it is more likely that old Mrs. Gentry will be grabbing her cantaloupe first thing Saturday morning, and she won't find the humor in seeing a snake in her fruit. Neither will our boss." Robert was a voice of reason.

"You're so boring." She grabbed her rubber snake from his shoulder and put it in the front of her apron.

"Better keep that thing hidden, Faith." Robert raised his eyebrows, still grinning ear to ear, just as their boss came by.

"Good morning, folks. Glad to see you. Everything Okay over here?" Mr. Macquire asked.

"Yes, sir," Robert said.

Faith watched Robert, loving to see him squirm and also delighted that he was such a sincerely good guy.

"How did last night go?" Mr. Macquire patted Robert on the shoulder.

"Good. Our team won." Robert nodded.

"And you? How did you do, young man?" His genuine smile mirrored Robert's.

"He scored twice, Mr. Macquire," Faith interrupted, beaming at Robert.

"Good job. Keep up the good work, kids, and remember—there are donuts in the break room," Mr. Macquire patted Robert's shoulder again as he walked away.

"Thank you, sir." Robert shook his head at Faith.

She read his mind. "That is why we don't plant snakes in the produce department."

Rolling her eyes, she smiled at him and trotted back to the break room.

Faith glided into her car as she had each morning for the next few months, pulling out the constraining band that held her hair. Shaking her head to free her locks to dance in the wind, she dappled a hint of gloss across her lips. Since she had been dating Robert for the past nine months, she felt more carefree than she ever had.

The more she learned about Robert, the more she respected him. Like her, he was the oldest child in his family. He happily accepted the weightiness of the responsibilities thrust upon him, setting an example to be successful for his three younger siblings. He told her about his kid sisters, and she could see how much he loved them.

Robert lived in a great neighborhood where he attended a private school. His parents worked to provide for their family.

His father was a manager at the manufacturing plant. His mother worked in the office of his private school, offsetting the cost for the family.

His parents expected Robert to work since the day he turned fourteen. Faith could see the benefits of having such high standards. *He sure is a go-getter and great with Johnny and the little girls.*

Unstoppable Truth: Character

Joy burst like the first sunrays after a heavy rain in Faith's life. Her newfound freedom was bubbling over and splashing onto Robert's world as well. He was a driven young man, and she brought balance to his hardcore work ethic. He taught her a few things about focusing on *her* future too.

The combination of these personalities was like a keg of dynamite. They had the potential to generate lives of high-spirited purpose.

Mordecai lived a life of magnanimous purpose as well. He embodied integrity, courage, strength, and sacrifice. Esther and her people were the benefactors of these unmatched qualities.

Character is refined in the fire. From the outside, watching a person make healthy decisions may look like it is second nature. Good, and might I say godly, choices mean building those muscles. Being a person of integrity, courage, strength, and sacrifice takes intentional heart work. These strengths are built one step and one decision at a time. Maneuvering small choices well is like placing one brick at a time onto a foundation and eventually having a life that withstands the hurricanes. The master carpenter of this inner-man work is the Spirit of God.

Mordecai was the perfect model of integrity where it really counted—on the battlefield of life. We will meet another person who portrayed integrity, courage, strength, and sacrifice in 1 Samuel. Hannah also teaches us how God hears the cries of our hearts and teaches us to trust Him and His timing. Let's learn from her and see how we too can be people with these same character qualities. Hannah inspires us to dare to believe God for big things.

Please read 1 Samuel 1:1–7.

1. Hannah was in despair. Her broken heart sought refuge in the only one who had the power to help.
   - Why was Hannah so distraught (1 Samuel 1:5)?
   - What made the matter even worse (1 Samuel 1:6)?
   - What emotion was evoked from this trial?

2. We see in 1 Samuel 1:7 that Elkanah and his wives traveled together every year to the house of the Lord. How did Peninnah treat Hannah on these trips?
   - Think about the situation Hannah was in. How must this barren woman have felt as she prepared to go again, traveling side by side with her fertile, bullying adversary?

3. Please read Psalm 37. What are we taught about fretting?
   - What happens to evil men/women (Psalm 37:2)?
   - What are we told to do instead (Psalm 37:3)?
   - As you seek to obey God, even in your trials, what does David promise (Psalm 37:4–5)?
   - How can we exercise our "trust" muscles when we are tempted to handle difficult situations (Psalm 37:27)?
   - What must we put in our hearts to be people of character (Psalm 37:31)?

4. Please read 1 Samuel 1:7–8 again. Peninnah's cruelty was taking a toll on Hannah. How does this impact her emotions?
   - Hannah's depressed condition did not totally give way to hopelessness. She still cried for help. She did not stay stuck as she courageously sought the Great Healer in this painful time in her life.
   - I love the example of her confident, earnest prayer!
   - Bless Elkanah, her husband, but he didn't get it. He couldn't fix it, as most good husbands would try. But bless him for trying. What question does he ask her? What did he apparently not understand?

5. Please read 1 Samuel 1:9–28. I love this part of Hannah's story because we see her godly example.
   - In 1 Samuel 1:9–16, how does Hannah show us what strength and courage look like?
   - In verses 15–17, look closely at what she says about her prayer. She is real! Though at first he was misguided, how did Eli's later words change Hannah's emotions? How does her faith prove her integrity?
   - Look at verses 19–28. What incredible sacrifice does Hannah make?

Reflection: Peninnah's bullying went on year after year. Have you ever had to endure hardship like that? If so, how did it make you feel? Were you ever so distraught that you couldn't eat and you couldn't stop crying? Maybe you are just the opposite.

Your stress led you to overeat. How do you react to extremely difficult trials?

Think about something you are currently fretting about or a situation when you have been distraught. What good came out of that?

How is Hannah's prayer an example to you? How might it impact your situation? Also, what truths could build your "courage muscles" as you study Psalm 37?

There was a time in my life when I was going through an exceedingly rough time at work. I had a Peninnah in my life after I had been promoted. Her harassment continued for years. I prayed about it every day. I also fretted about it—until one night I awoke at 2:00 a.m. and began to play that crummy tape in my mind again. The Spirit of God spoke one simple phrase to my heart: "Fretting is not faith."

At that moment I knew I needed to turn that tape of fear off for good! That night I exercised those faith muscles and those muscles have only gotten stronger. When I am worried, I pray to God, who can make a barren woman a mama, and I leave it with Him.

Chapter 4
Vulnerability

The extreme heat of summer began to give way to the cool of autumn, and the leaves began to turn vibrant golds, oranges, and burgundy tones. Robert and Faith's relationship blossomed like the bright mums in front of the weathered farmhouse, and the transformation echoed the change in their feelings for one another.

Faith became Robert's greatest cheerleader at his football games.

He loved having her by his side. Sunday afternoons became filled with long drives, adventurous hikes in the country, and regular visits to their favorite burger place.

Faith's laughter filled each room she entered with needful warmth. She captured Robert's heart.

He, a driven, diligent worker, grew more fascinated by this fly-by-the-seat-of-your-pants, joyous, golden-haired beauty. He needed her genuine, lively personality. Her good looks and tender heart were a bonus.

They were both raised with family values where words like *integrity*, *honesty*, and *character* were uttered over mashed potatoes and meatloaf, and their budding love seemed to be providential.

One evening after Robert's team experienced a devastating loss, he got into his car and melted like butter in his seat. Faith sat next to him, waiting for the right words to say to him. "I can't believe I threw that right into their hands." He threw the pass in the direction of his receiver, but the safety must have read his eyes and jumped the route, making the interception. Robert blamed himself. The loss would guarantee that they would not make it to state.

This was the first time Faith would see Robert heartbroken. She listened to him as he chided himself, replaying what he should have done differently. Faith respected him for that. He was a stand-up guy, but sometimes he could put too much pressure on himself.

The next day after work they went for a picnic at a park in town. Grabbing the football that Robert carried in his trunk, they tossed it around in the sunlight. As they sat on a blanket afterward, Faith felt that she could trust Robert with her family's most devastating story.

In the last several months Robert had picked up on the fact that deep hurt hovered over Faith's family. The dark fog had formed over the battle brought on by her mother's alcoholism.

Faith explained how confusion filled their house. Even from her earliest memories, she recalled coming home to a mother who had been with her closest companion, vodka, all day.

Without an ounce of bitterness, Faith told Robert of the typical afternoons when she and her siblings would come home from school and her mom would be hammered. This forced Faith and Johnny into the role of lifting her from the kitchen floor and placing her frail frame into bed.

Faith went on to explain that in those days, her father would come in late from work at his office in town. The responsibilities were piled on Faith and Johnny's shoulders, like a constraining yoke.

Trusting Robert with her story, Faith confided that as she was preparing to start high school, her mother was being prepared for her casket. Life would never be the same for the George family.

Robert loved her even more for trusting him with her story.

Unstoppable Truth: Vulnerability

Brené Brown, author of *Daring Greatly: How the Courage to Be Vulnerable Transforms the Way We Live, Love, Parent, and Lead*, says vulnerability is defined as "uncertainty, risk, and emotional exposure." That's life, isn't it? Especially if we want to live a life of authentic relationships.

We have to walk into uncertainty and go places we have never gone before. We have to open up and trust people with our stories. We have to take risks and reach for goals that we think might be out of our grasp. And probably the hardest of all, we have to take a chance at emotional exposure.

This last one was by far the hardest for me—putting my heart out there and giving others the chance to stomp all over it. But I also knew they might hold it tenderly. I made myself take that chance. But to be honest, when I first did it with almost strangers, it was painful. Really painful, and I didn't do it well. At all.

As I was earning my master's degree, a significant part of my learning was training as a coach. We, as a class, told our story, including where we had been, who we were, and what we hoped to become. As God often does, my spiritual life collided with this very emotional, educational part of my life. As I became a member of a new church and joined a Bible study, one of the expectations was to give my testimony. Both were scheduled within a week of one another, which was a pretty big hint that God was stretching my vulnerability muscles!

In the Bible study it was my turn to tell my story. Not wanting to hurt anyone, especially those who I loved, I chose my words carefully. I was cautious of what I shared about my own vulnerabilities. Those details noted my deepest pain that was wrapped up in hurtful choices others had made toward me. I took the easy way out and just decided to tell the group about all the times God had shown up in my life, and I was vague about my own sinfulness and the sins people had committed against me.

The next Sunday evening after three women told their stories of pain, adultery, divorce, and homelessness, I felt the Lord impress on my heart.

"You have robbed them," He said to me. "They gave all, and you gave almost nothing."

So I told my own story—the good, the bad, the ugly, and the hard to hear. And the truth freed me, just as the Word promises it will.

Then in a class I took for my master's degree, I shared what had brought me to this place in which I earned my master's degree in management. I let them see my pain from brokenness, pain from rejection, and pain from being an outcast in the community I had served and loved. Real stinkin'-hard pain. Truths that are hard for folks to wrap their minds around.

I uncovered the transformation of my life of homelessness after my divorce to my goal to prove God's promises are true. My classmates silently tried to reconcile my put-together appearance with my recently shattered past.

"That was good to know," said one of my fellow classmates. "I would have never guessed. You taught me to look deeper than at the surface at people." He extended his hand to grip mine.

Being vulnerable hurts like the dickens. And it heals.

Being real helps others to be real as well.

It took courage for Robert to be vulnerable with Faith about his failure. He took the plunge, desiring a deeper relationship with her. Isn't that the stuff that the best fairy tales are made of in which the guy puts his heart on the line for the girl?

Life is full of backstories—mine, Faith's, Esther's, and yours.

This is why we need to entrench ourselves into the depths of God's Word. Well, this is why I need to entrench myself into my loving Abba Father's Word. The answers are in the deep! Let's dive in together!

Robert, Faith, Esther, and I all had something in common. We were all in vulnerable situations. Let's look at the lessons Esther learned and see how the Bible has answers for each one of us.

1. Please read Esther 3.

    The king's choice to honor Haman would prove to be detrimental to Esther and the Jewish people. It would put them in a fatally vulnerable position. People's lousy, uninformed choices can do that.

    Mordecai's character and integrity put him in a vulnerable position as well. Having character when you are in an unhealthy environment can also do that. Sadly. When the king put Haman in this prestigious position, how did the other officials respond (Esther 3:1–2)?

    - Please look again at Esther 3:2–6. What was Haman's plan?

2. Let's take a gander at Esther 3:8–9. How did Haman manipulate King Ahasuerus? And does Haman explain who these people are? Manipulation often leaves out the whole story, doesn't it?

- What is Haman called (Esther 3:10)?
- What lousy permission did the king give Haman (Esther 3:11)?

3. The plot thickens. Let's look deeply at Esther 3:12.
   - Who did they write the script to?
   - How many provinces did this include (Esther 1:1)? (That is a lot of places and more importantly a lot of exceedingly vulnerable people!)
   - What was the desired outcome that the orders would bring about?
   - Who would it impact?

4. Can you share a time when you have been in a vulnerable position (it can be life and death or another less threatening situation) when the options could have proven to be destructive to your well-being?

5. Did you reach out to anyone and share what you were going through? Did it help or bring you peace?

The beauty from ashes that is Faith's story: Faith's mom did not know where to turn as she went through her difficulties. And as Faith's father faced being a widower and a single father, Mr. George had no idea where to turn either. In the next section we will see how God's hand was on this family and how God would use difficult circumstances to bring them the healing balm they needed.

Dear Lord,

Thank You for loving us each so much. Please be with this delightful reader. May this be his or her prayer.

Lord, if there is a part of my story I should share, please help me to tell it! As I desire to grow in You, may I also grow in a healthy community with others. Lord, I pray for a safe, honorable person I can trust with my truth, regardless of how sad, hard, or even how wonderful and inspiring it is.

Lord, I know You are in the messiness of life, and You want me to be there for others also. Thank You for being the God who sees, hears, and heals. Thank You, sweet Savior, for being all those things and more. My love for You is ever-growing as I trust You more and more. Thank You for being the hero of my story!

In Jesus's name, (*Your name*)

Chapter 5

Change

"What will we do after we clear the table?" Victoria asked. The family was finishing the chocolate chip pancakes and bacon, a favorite for Sunday brunch.

"You pick." Robert leaned toward her. With his huge index finger, he tenderly tapped her on her wrinkled nose.

"Hey, kid, you don't have to do that," Daddy assured Robert as he passed him the bottle of maple syrup.

"No, it's fine, sir. Faith and I enjoy it." Robert nodded as his lips turned upward, letting her father know they were on board.

"You're it!" Robert's touching Victoria's curly golden mop ignited screeching and giggles as her tennies pounded into the fenced pasture. Her pigtails danced joyously with each stride.

"I'm going to get you!" Robert growled and exaggerated his body movements toward her. His frame loomed, spinning his long arms around her head.

Playing tag with her siblings and Robert was Faith's favorite.

Faith liked to play hide and seek, especially when she and Robert hid together and would sneak a peck in until their spot was discovered.

"You're like another brother." Mary said to Robert as they refreshed themselves over vanilla ice cream and sprinkles.

"No, more like a best friend," Johnny interrupted, capturing Robert's glance.

"True." Robert smiled and gently smacked Johnny's muscled arm. Then as he held out his fist, they pounded one another.

The feelings were mutual for Robert's family concerning Faith too. The first time Robert swung the door open, Faith was met by a perfectly put-together hostess, yet, still in her robe.

"You caught me." Mrs. Ryan's chuckle filled the room. "I was still doing my housework." She smiled at Robert, offering a warm glare. "Why didn't you tell me?" She extended her arms toward Faith, squeezed her tightly, and pulled her into her soft, mushy orbit.

Unprepared for a bear hug, Faith stiffened with her arms locked next to her sides. Her eyes widened as she searched for Robert as if she were asking him to save her.

Mrs. Ryan touched Faith's arms, then gently pressed Faith back so she could take in the full view. "And why didn't you tell me just how pretty she is?"

"Mom, I did tell you." Robert raised his eyebrows, glanced at Faith, and shook his head as his eyes asked for forgiveness. "Faith, this is my mother." His hand covered her shoulder and he nodded to this tidal wave of energy as he shook his head and grinned. "Mom, this is Faith."

Faith learned to welcome Robert's mother's hugs, getting over the initial discomfort of such a bubbly gust of vitality. The kisses at the front door eventually made her feel at home on Saturday afternoons. On one such afternoon, with their textbooks wide open, note cards out, and computers glowing, laughter between Faith and Robert echoed from every space they settled.

"Let's go for a run and take Goldie. She needs to get out." Faith closed her book, rested her chin on her open hands, and looked expectantly at Robert across the table.

"I better finish this first." Robert tried to put the brakes on her free spirit.

"Your homework will be here all evening, and the sun will be gone in a couple of hours." Her crinkled eyes and nose framed her sparkling blue eyes. She tilted her head and melted his heart.

"True." He placed his pencil in the center of his book, stood, and reached for Faith's hand. "Come on, Goldie." He bent over and rubbed the retriever's back. She bounced up and wagged her tail, beating Faith and Robert to the door.

Mrs. Ryan's heart fluttered. Knowing they were too enamored of one another to look back and catch her looking, she scooted to the kitchen and ogled them through the window. Placing her manicured hand on her heart, she fixed her eyes on her ambitious son as he stretched his arm around Faith's shoulder, pulling her near. Spinning to stir the garlic, onion, and Italian spices into the tomatoey spaghetti sauce, she was grateful for Faith's spirit. It balanced Robert's determined temperament.

Gripping the leash, Robert and Faith scurried out of sight.

Mrs. Ryan had been concerned that Robert took being at the top of his class, his job, his role as the oldest child, and his future goals way too seriously. Then she pondered her husband's words after a hard-fought victory on the field. "The boy's grind-it-out work ethic has put him on the fast track to success." She knew Robert's accomplishments also eased the heart-tightening weight that Mr. Ryan put on himself to provide for his family.

She secured the band on her apron, lifted the spoon from the pot, and dipped her finger inside. *Dee-lish!* Plopping the spoon into the bubbles in the sink, she dashed from the kitchen to get dressed, grateful that Robert was happy and that dinner was ready.

A year behind Robert, Faith was still researching possibilities for college since the bulk of her days in high school thus far had been consumed with cleaning, cooking, and administering homework around the dining room table. She hadn't had the time to concentrate on her own goals, and as a result, universities were not beating down her door. She wouldn't have changed it for the world, though. The little ones had needed her. She was considering two-year colleges nearby, even though things were different at home now.

Faith was not the only one dating in the George household. One Friday evening after football season was over, Faith was the one serving dinner. Mr. George had run upstairs and changed from his suit into jeans and a button-down shirt. He kissed each child goodnight and cautioned them to be good. Glancing away, Faith felt her heart sink into her chest as she smelled the aftershave he used to wear when her mother was still alive.

Mutual friends from work had introduced them. He kept it from the younger kids at first, not wanting to disrupt the new normal he had worked to secure for the last couple of years. Faith had to be trusted with his secret since she needed to cover for him when he went on dates.

Elisa had a one-and-a-half-year-old little girl of her own. *That was interesting, crazy interesting,* Faith thought.

After a few weeks Faith assumed that Johnny must have figured it out, but he never asked, so she never told.

Her dad eventually introduced Elisa to "the herd," as he called them. Faith wondered if the high-class ex-model would soften the edges and maybe change daddy's home-grown vocabulary.

One Saturday evening Faith, figuring this was going to be a long-term relationship, confided in Robert. "Daddy and the younger kids don't need me." She swiped the uninvited trickle from her cheek, turning her head away from Robert in the parked car.

"Naw, it's just different now." Robert turned fully toward her and waited for her to glance back.

"Daddy has changed our family. I . . ."

"What do you think of Elisa?" Robert turned his long torso, inhaled a quiet breath, and looked Faith directly in the eyes.

"I suppose I like her, but it's weird." Faith turned away from Robert and sought solace in the fluffy white clouds above the fields.

"Weird because of your mom?" Robert sometimes asked way too many questions for Faith's liking.

"I don't want to talk about it anymore." Faith sucked in all the air from her side of the car and looked Robert in the eye. "It doesn't matter anyway; it's his decision." The resolve in her tone didn't match her quivering lips.

Robert couldn't feel Faith's pain, but he wished he could take it away. Scooting toward her seat, he reached his arms around her.

Immediately loosening her stiff body, Faith melted into Robert's embrace. Being near him made her feel as the shattered pieces had a place to rest.

UNSTOPPABLE PEACE: *A STORY OF FAITH*

Unstoppable Truth: Change

Change is often one of the hardest things any of us go through. Even good changes can bring stress. The not knowing makes us feel a loss of control and often makes our future feel insecure. I have felt that in personal and professional situations. New homes, new jobs, and new relationships can all come with a pinch of strain as we move forward. Faith was feeling it, and Esther did too. Esther's example in her newly acquired, God-given role gave me what I needed so many times. Especially as my marriage took a turn for the worse.

Change reminds us that we are not in control. What we do with that realization can be life-altering.

While change is often good, sometimes the good is uncovered only by strenuous heart-wrenching circumstances that feel unbearably bad. Faith, Mordecai, Esther, and I have been forced to embrace this epiphany.

Please read Esther 4:1–14.

1. From Esther 4:1–3, what was Mordecai's reaction to the news he and the other Jews had gotten? Please do a Google search, or if you have Bible resources, unearth the significance of sackcloth and ashes and tearing one's clothes.
    - Based on what you learned, why did Mordecai react this way?
    - Why didn't he go directly to Esther (verse 2)?
    - How did the other Jews react (verse 3)?

2. When I took the CliftonStrengths finder assessment, one of my top five strengths was positivity, and then my enneagram reinforced it, dubbing me a seven. I always look for the positive in every situation. I have learned that sometimes that means denying the reality of what is actually going on. I think that may be what we are seeing here in Esther 4:4 when Esther thought a new outfit might cover Mordecai's apparent distress. Or maybe she desired that he not reveal his nationality. Or as I have to remind myself often too, she may have been in disbelief of the evil that some people (Haman) were capable of.

   Regardless of the reason, Esther was not facing the state of affairs and decision that she, and only she, needed to make. Can you understand how she may have been feeling?

3. When Hathach (from verse 6) went out into the square, where did he meet with Mordecai?
   - Why is this significant?
   - What did Mordecai tell him (verse 7)?
   - What did he give him to give to Esther (verse 8)?
   - What request did he make of Esther (verse 8)?

I love Mordecai. He was a man of character and responsibility. First he raised his cousin, always expecting her to do right and to be treated with dignity. Then he demanded that she in turn remember that life was not all about her beautiful self. Man, do we need some more people like Mordecai in leadership today!

4. When Hathach went back to Esther and told her everything (Esther 4:9), what did Esther say she feared (verses 10–11)?

5. What was the profound warning that Mordecai gave Esther in verses 13–14? What needed to change?

> *"And who knows but that you have come to your royal position for such a time as this?"*
> Esther 4:14 (NIV)

What significant position did Faith have, based on our storyline? What changes in her life had brought that about?

Reflection: My precious friend, has some painful or life-altering challenge given you a special position that God can use if you allow Him to? Please ponder what He is doing in your life. Can you see His hand in it?

Is He trying to bring about a big change in you? What is it? I encourage you to take a moment and write out a prayer to our sovereign God. Be honest with Him. Ask Him to show you what to do next and how to put yourself aside for the good of others.

Dear sovereign God,

Chapter 6

Acceptance

The next afternoon at work, Faith looked up and saw Elisa striding toward her. *What . . . ? Where can I hide?* She bent over, gathering an array of apples and her thoughts, trying to put both in order.

"Hi, sweetie." Elisa took a deep breath. "Looks like you're hard at work." Her smile dissipated as she took in the distress she read on Faith's face.

"Yes, can I help you?" Faith stood, consciously trying to put on a smile while brushing the dust on her pants. *Oh, my gosh, I look horrible.* Especially in comparison to the life-sized Barbie in front of her.

"Can I treat you to a sandwich?" Elisa smiled, biting her lip.

Faith glanced over Elisa's shoulder at the huge clock above the registers and noticed it was lunchtime. "Well, I usually eat with

Robert," she started to explain until she saw Elisa's eyes drop to the floor. "But I guess that will work." Faith's heart was racing as she glanced at her dad's friend. Fidgeting with the gold band on her purse, Faith knew she should go. She figured it wasn't about eating anyway.

As they sat across the table from one another, Elisa's shining white teeth were perfectly framed with a carnation pink lipstick. "How are you, Faith?" She leaned in, bowed her head, and rested her chin on the top of her hands. Her manicured fingertips touched one another.

"I'm Okay." Faith noticed that the pink blouse and white pearls looked perfect with her ironed creased jeans, which looked brand new. Blinking, she nibbled on her bottom lip and silently glanced toward each corner of the room.

Elisa reached down and lifted a greasy fry to her teeth, not touching her perfectly lined lips.

Faith picked up her roast beef sandwich, dipped it in the hot cup of broth, and took a bite. She noticed Elisa's blouse rushing in and out like the sea, acknowledging they were both nervous. Setting her sandwich next to the sliced pickle on her plate, she saw the discomfort on Elisa's face. "How are *you*?" She conceded concern.

"This is a big change for both of us, huh?" Elisa's words proved that she got it.

"I guess so." Faith's lips unknowingly lifted on both sides, and she nodded.

"If you ever need to talk, I'm here. I really do understand."

Faith believed her. Looking at her crossed long legs and her plate with one missing fry, Faith realized why she had asked her out to lunch. She saw the tenderness of the woman her daddy was falling in love with.

"Thank you. I will . . . someday." Faith glanced away from the table, ordering her tears to stay where they belonged.

They chatted for the next fifteen minutes about work, school, and the little ones, but not about Faith's dad. Before the Saturday crowd could take over the diner, they stood in unison, pushing the chairs back toward the table.

Tossing the rest of her fries into the trash, Elisa turned and connected with Faith's eyes. "If you want to go out with Robert, I will take Chloe to the farm and help your dad with the others this evening."

"Thank you." Faith looked down, battling her sense of responsibility with her own wishes.

"May I?" Elisa asked with both arms spread out.

Faith nodded, and Elisa, in one motion, swept her into her arms. Faith fought the yearning of wanting to lay her head on the woman's soothing, gentle shoulder as she felt the brush of Elisa's soft cheek.

"Thank you for lunch," Faith whispered as they both pulled away and looked one another in the eye. Faith wondered if this would be the first of many. She understood Daddy's choice now.

Summer turned to fall, and the chilly air, the subdued golden, amber, and bronze leaves were illuminated by the sun. Like a brilliant orange ball, it hovered over the steeple of the small white church. It was the perfect backdrop for Mr. George and Elisa's wedding. Faith and Johnny faced the intimate group of family members and a few friends as they stood next to the pastor. Their father and Elisa clutched one another's hands. They each took the hand of their own toddling daughters dressed in soft peach dresses. Dropping crème-colored rose petals, the girls walked down the center of the room together. After exchanging their vows, and accepting the congratulations from the guests, the newlyweds scooped up their newly combined family and headed to the farm to prepare for what they hoped to be a normal home for this merged cluster.

Home took on a new meaning for Faith.

Every day children scampered in the kitchen while Elisa brewed oatmeal on the stove and packed lunches, lifting Faith's burden. Her new stepmom smiled one day, gently massaging Faith's shoulders as she leaned into the refrigerator to grab a jug of milk—a gentle reminder to let Faith know she could relax. Like a candle in a dim cave, Elisa decorated each room with kindness.

Unstoppable Truth: Acceptance

Life was different, whether or not Faith liked it. Her father was also transformed. Faith had the same choice we all have when someone we love goes through a metamorphosis; she could fight it and become discontent, angry, and bitter, or she could accept it. Accepting it doesn't mean we won't ache for the past, but it does allow us to look forward to the future. Especially if we discern the handprint of God in the future.

The most quoted verse from the book of Esther is found in chapter four, verse 14 (NIV): "And who knows but that you have come to your royal position for such a time as this?" Let's remember why Mordecai uttered these words. He was alerting Esther, asking her to consider why God would call her to this royal position.

My dear friend, please consider the same question for yourself. Why has God put you on the earth? He has placed you in your career, in your family, in your school, and in your community for a reason. He has a purpose for you! Let's dig a bit and see what that purpose may be.

1. Please Read Jeremiah 33:3. When we are not sure why God would put us in certain places or circumstances, what does this verse indicate we should do?

2. There are times when we cannot fathom why God is doing certain things. What should we remember from Isaiah 55:8?

3. One of the first verses a godly friend impressed upon my heart was Romans 8:28. It was when I first began to trust in Jesus. My childhood was blotted with trauma and trials. This verse gave me hope. What hope do you see in this verse?

4. When my teenage daughter was moving over 1,000 miles away from her childhood home, a sweet chum she had known her entire life etched Romans 8:18 on a little scrap of paper. Please write this verse out below.

5. God created us to be people of dignity, beauty, and purpose. Life has a way of stripping those qualities from us. Instead of losing hope, think about Esther, Modecai, and Hannah. How should we, as people who trust Christ, react to difficult trials?

Mordecai built his character muscles long before Esther became queen. We will see those steps a bit later.

Chapter 7

Remembering

"Do you have plans this evening?" Elisa asked.

"What?" Faith glanced up at her stepmother.

"What are you doing after school?"

"After I do homework with the little ones, I'll do my own."

"I can help the others in case you want to go to the library and study or hang out with friends." Elisa smiled and leaned against the sink.

Taking it all in, Faith wondered if this is what it felt like to be a typical high school girl without the extra responsibilities of her younger siblings. As she slowly lifted the spoon to her lips, thoughts of her classmates standing around laughing and joking about the previous weekend's escapades reminded her that her previous life was not the typical story of a teenager.

"Hmm, hadn't thought about it." Fatih grabbed a napkin from the center of the table and dabbed the corners of her mouth.

"If you make plans, just give me a call today. I'll be home." Elisa stroked Faith's ponytail. "You look pretty today."

Faith sat quietly as Elisa went to check on the rest of the children's progress. *What do I want to do?*

When Faith came in from the library that evening, she scooped up some clam chowder that Elisa had left warming on the stove. Sitting down at the wooden table across from her, Elisa asked what she was thinking about colleges. Faith was grateful to have someone to share this time with. Her mind wandered from reality to the scene she wished she was in. *What would Mother have thought about me going to college?*

"Your father tells me that your mother was very smart." Elisa smiled, not having an ounce of insecurity in her statuesque frame.

Faith nodded, trying to figure out how Elisa could read her thoughts. Faith had come to appreciate Elisa's wisdom, even if it unsettled her sometimes. Most of all, Faith treasured seeing Elisa tell her father that he was a good man when he came home from work. Meeting him at the door, she would stretch her long legs and back to kiss him on the cheek.

After breakfast on many mornings, Faith watched Elisa run a brush through the younger girls' long hair. As she finished, she would place her hands on their cheeks, smooching each one on her nose or forehead, telling her how stunning she was. The house smelled of the scents of fresh bread and echoed with the humming tunes from the sound of music. Elisa's little girl, Chloe, and the George family were blended like chocolate syrup into a shake; they became inseparably one.

Remembering her own mother's laughter and love had been difficult in the last couple of years. The end of her life was overshadowed by the empty bottles and staggering falls. Other than Johnny, the little ones had few recollections. Faith was determined to tell them the few sweet stories of holidays and celebrations so they wouldn't forget her.

"Mom always loved Halloween," Faith reported to them as they were deciding on what to be late in October.

"Did she ever dress up?" Margo asked, hoping to hold onto the woman who was becoming more and more of a memory.

"No, but she liked to help us decide what to be. One year she told Johnny he should be a farmer. Do you remember that?" Faith turned to her brother.

At first he beamed. He liked to remember his mom. Then he pursed his lips and hung his head. "I remember."

Then in a whisper he added, "I wanted to be a football player, but I also wanted to make Mom happy. That night when Dad came home, we all talked about it at the dinner table. Dad told us about Tom Osborne, a former college and professional football player who went on to coach at Nebraska. So I went as a Nebraska football player."

"Yeah, Johnny. Mom loved helping you put together that costume with the big N on your chest." Faith looked at the little ones.

"I remember." Johnny wiped his mouth with his napkin, then scooted his chair out and walked away. The back door closed with an echo behind him.

"Those stories make Johnny sad," Margo whispered. "But I like to hear about Mommy."

It is good to remember our mother. She loved us all so much, Faith wanted to say, *especially Johnny,* but she didn't. She knew that the little ones wouldn't understand. But Faith was old enough to know that Johnny's tall, handsome frame and sweet disposition were so much like their daddy's that Johnny was Mom's favorite. Johnny knew it too.

Now they had Elisa. But they would never forget their mother. Never, Faith vowed to herself. Elisa brought joy into their home with laughter, stories, and good-night kisses. She also made holidays and birthday celebrations enjoyable for family and friends.

"Victoria, shall we have your class over for a hayride for Halloween?" Elisa asked.

"Can we?" Victoria shrieked with excitement.

"Sure." Elisa's wheels were turning.

"Actually, kids, how about if you all invite some friends?" Elisa said. "We will have a fall festival out here at the farm." Elisa and the kids started formulating a plan immediately.

When Daddy got home, Elisa told him about the party and the part he would play for the big day, especially the hayrides.

"Sorry, guys. I have so much going on at the office that I don't think that will work." Daddy burst the party bubble.

Almost immediately after Dad and Elisa married, work took center stage for him, as when Mom was alive. When the children woke up, he had already finished the farm work. As they all sat at the breakfast table, they would hear his long stride come down the wooden staircase. He replaced his dirty boots and Carhartt jacket with black leather shoes and a suit. Daddy's transformation was like that of Superman. The outside world saw the hero who saved the day at the office. But if the family could stay awake in the late evenings, they saw a hard-working farmer sliding his boots off and slumping over his plate. Faith admired him for always being such a hard worker, but she missed him, especially since he had made such an effort to cook, play football, and be home after their mother had died.

Elisa respected his hard work too. She knew it made him happy, but she was determined that he would be a part of his kids' lives.

"Remember—I want to talk later about the party, dear. I want the kids to have some fun," Elisa said as Daddy slid on his Black leather shoes to leave the next morning.

"Tonight." He smiled, taking in the full view of his new bride in her soft pink robe.

"Be good today." He tussled each one of the kids' hair as they sat around the breakfast table. Elisa got a gentle kiss on the cheek as she scooped steaming oatmeal into Johnny's bowl. Even in a robe and with no makeup on, she was stunning.

"See you tonight." She returned his kiss, patting his upper back, bringing a smile to Daddy's face.

Elisa had changed everything at home.

Unstoppable Truth: Remembering

Esther needed to remember that God had allowed her to be there for such a time as this. God had enabled her beauty to open doors to new responsibilities. Her outward appearance was not her defining attribute; it was her courage, strength, integrity, and sacrifice that would make her a woman of memorable dignity—an unselfish woman whom her people needed.

Watching her father with Elisa brought back so many uninvited memories to Faith. Remembrances of Christmas trees her mother decorated with bundles of brightly wrapped gifts. Recollections of birthday parties and perfectly decorated cakes designed by her mother. The aroma of vibrant lilacs she brought in from the yard. If Faith really concentrated, she could still hear her mother's laughter. She had the deepest, most sincere laugh.

Though remembering tore her heart into shreds, she made herself remember every now and then, telling herself she could never let herself forget.

My beautiful friend, is there value in ruminating on the past? What does God tell us about remembering? Is there something you need to allow yourself to remember? Or maybe there are seasons of your life you need to choose to forget.

1. Please read Joshua 4. God teaches us the value of remembering in this chapter.
   - What directions did the Lord give to Joshua (Joshua 4:1–5)?
   - Why did God want Joshua to take up the stones (verses 6–7)?
   - In Joshua 4:24 we see the importance of remembering God's faithfulness in our trials.

Please write Joshua 4:24 below.

2. Please read 2 Corinthians 10:3–5. We who trust in Christ are urged by the apostle Paul to live differently than the world around us. What must we remember from this passage?
   - Even when our thoughts seem to be in control, especially thoughts like worry, insecurity, or unforgiveness, what does 2 Corinthians 10:5 assure us of?
   - What thoughts do you want to change?

3. Since we have the power through God to be in control of our thoughts, please read Philippians 4:8 and make a list below of what we should be thinking about.

4. In Philippians 3:13–15, Paul gives us some solid advice, saying some things should not be remembered; we should train ourselves to forget. What past hurts do you need to forget so you can move forward? What sins do you need to repent of so you can move past them? Write a prayer below if you would like or simply pray to God, but make sure you give Him your hurts and sins once and for all!

Reflection: My beloved friend, the truths shared in this chapter have changed my life. As we desire to please God as new creations in Christ, the greatest gift we can give ourselves is to forget the former things, especially the negative, and move forward. I pray that if you struggle with this, you will continue to meditate on and memorize some of the verses shared in this chapter.

Chapter 8

Choices

While Robert was still around for his last year of high school, he and Faith spent most of their free time together. They went to dances and movies, having a blast. Faith loved it when he put down his books long enough to enjoy their weekends. She was all about the fun. Robert was all about achievements.

Robert's senior year was consumed with extra-hard classes, including his fourth year of French. He was mature and reasonable, and sometimes even boring, Faith thought. But she loved him and believed him when he told her his efforts would be rewarded in their future. Robert was not like other guys in high school. Faith's dad called him driven. And he was.

Robert was right. His hard work did pay off, and he was getting a lot of offers from colleges. His grades in high school set him up for countless scholarships and even greater opportunities to travel abroad to study.

"I don't want you to go," Faith said to Robert one night after a football game.

"If it weren't for you, it would be easy to go to France." Robert refocused his gaze from the front windshield to Faith and hugged her. "This is so good for my future, and something I just can't believe is happening, but leaving you kills me."

Faith started to cry, and then she made herself say what she knew Robert needed to hear. "I am happy for you, and I know you will be amazing."

They kissed good-night and promised to wait for one another.

The next day Faith gripped the steering wheel, telling herself she would be Okay. She tried to believe Elisa's words that it would be an adventure for both her and Robert. When she drove up, Robert's dad was hoisting the most enormous suitcase she had ever seen into the trunk. Robert and his mother were coming out of the front door of his parent's house.

"Just in time, sweetie." Robert's mom squeezed Faith. "Are you Okay? I know you'll miss him."

Faith nodded, looking into the woman's eyes, then glanced away.

Faith and Robert sat in the back seat. With intertwined fingers, each of them wiped away tears. Not able to look at one another, they both knew that the trickles would lead to a gush of uncontainable emotions. From the front seat, Robert's mother went on and on about staying in contact. Robert's dad was silent until arriving at the airport.

"Remember all your hard work, son. This is what you have

worked to achieve." His dad inhaled a deep breath. As he gave Robert a quick hug and a pat on the back, he glanced at Robert's mom. "Now don't make him cry." He warned her as much for himself as for Robert.

"Let me know how you are, who your roommates are, and about your dorm," his mother said. "Please remember to send pictures so I can experience my oldest as a grown man." She reached up for a hug.

As Robert's eyes met Faith's, they wiped each other's tears, and Robert tenderly kissed her on the forehead.

"Remember me" was all Faith could get out.

Robert nodded. His shoulders shook as he walked toward his airplane.

This day was the second hardest in Faith's life thus far. She felt the loss of her mother all over again. *I hate goodbyes.* The ache of unhealed wounds resurfaced.

Work wasn't the same. Because she and Robert were a contented duo, always competing, laughing, and having lunch with each other, she didn't have any other close friends at work. For the first time since starting to date Robert, her employment felt tedious. She would dedicate herself to her responsibilities at school, home, and the grocery store and just try to exist until Robert came back.

One Saturday Leasa, a coworker, asked if she wanted to take their lunch break together.

"Sure." Even though Faith didn't know her well, she wanted to be kind.

"Robert's away at college, right?" Leasa nibbled the crust from around her sandwich.

"He left about a month ago." Faith looked at the peanut butter cookies Elisa had put in her lunch. Faith's favorite.

"That sucks," Leasa said. She looked like an all-American girl.

Her response surprised Faith. "Yeah, it's pretty rough. I miss him a lot." Faith took a chance at being more vulnerable than she wanted to be.

"I bet." Leasa seemed annoyed. "When my big sister's boyfriend went away to college," Leasa said, chomping into the center of her sandwich, "he met a new girl the first weekend he was there." Leasa pursed her lips and shook her head in disgust. "My sister was a wreck until she met someone else."

"It's not like that with Robert and me. We're waiting for one another," Faith whispered, wrapping up her last cookie. "We love each other."

"We'll see." Leasa tossed the rest of her lunch into her bag and headed back into the store.

Faith thought about Leasa's words all day. She reminded herself that she and Robert talked once a week and even sent messages to each other throughout the day. *It's not like that for us. It's not like that for us. It's not like that for us.* Maybe if she said it to herself often enough, she would believe it.

As the year trotted on, Faith tried to stay positive. She was glad it was her senior year. Making final decisions about college, she was not the exemplary student that Robert was, so schools weren't banging down her door. The needs of the family, especially in the past four years, left little time for extra-curricular activities. There would be no college scholarship offers for her, and all she wanted was to be with Robert.

Family life had new stresses, with so many little ones around and her father getting used to his new wife. Faith noticed that even though Elisa was a great mom to her new kids, she looked more exhausted each day and got annoyed at Mr. George's very long workdays.

"Honey, you're too busy. This is not good for our new family." Elisa was calm, considering how irritated Faith imagined she must be. She could sometimes hear them through the wall that separated her bedroom from theirs.

"I know, but it won't be like this forever," he promised.

"You're right. It won't be like this forever. We need to make some changes. I love you. I married you to be your wife and partner, as well as us raising the kids. Together."

Elisa wasn't like Mom. She didn't drink. She was also different in the way she talked to Daddy.

Faith was surprised at the memories that flooded her mind and heart. The conversations her parents had had crept through the walls as well.

When her mother was alive, her father would leave the house at four in the morning, do farm chores, and then leave for work. Coming home late in the evening was his way of life, except for the brief time after Faith's mother died and before Elisa entered the house.

When Faith was little, her parents would argue, and nothing would change. That's when Faith noticed that her mother started drinking after breakfast.

This particular morning Daddy was quiet. What would happen? Faith wished she could slip out of her room without making a sound. No one talked to Daddy like this.

"Let's talk tonight after the kids go to bed," Faith heard Elisa say through the wall.

Faith headed out of her room, trying to scramble outside as

soon as she could. She and Elisa entered the kitchen at the same time. Elisa, still as beautiful as a movie star, held her chest in and smiled, trying to act as if nothing had occurred.

What might happen next? Memories of Faith's father talking to her mother about her drinking were carved in her memories. She wished she could erase the engraved words.

Faith went to work and tried to stay busy, hoping the clanking of the cans would drown out the noise in her head. *What if Elisa leaves? The little ones will be abandoned again. Daddy will be lost. And what about college? He will need me back here.*

"Hey, Faith—do you want to hang out after work?" Leasa asked, interrupting the racket in Faith's head.

"Um, sure. I guess." She had no excuse not to. Besides, she still held out hope for a normal life.

"Follow me. I'll show you where I live."

As Leasa pulled out of the parking lot, Faith followed close behind. As they crossed onto the street, each small home looked like tiny matching Monopoly houses. Flags in front and driveways led to one-car garages. The neighborhood looked like what you would see on TV. Each yard was impeccably manicured. Mums and gourds of all colors lined the front of each home.

Faith cautiously got out of her car, following Leasa.

"Hi, Gram and Gramps," Leasa said as she opened the door. The aroma of banana bread hit their faces.

"Hi, sweetie," they said in unison. They looked at Faith as if she were a lost kitten, surprised to see her wandering in, then both stood to greet her.

"This is Faith, a friend from work." Leasa pointed to her while grabbing a piece of banana bread from the china plate on the table.

"Welcome, Faith," Leasa's gramps looked a lot like what she had imagined her dad would look like when he got old.

"Banana bread, sweetheart?" asked Leasa's gram.

As Leasa went to her room and changed her clothes, her grandparents made Faith feel at home.

"Where is your mom?" Faith asked Leasa as they drove back toward town in Leasa's car.

"She's a piece of work. I don't want to talk about it." Leasa ended the conversation abruptly.

Leasa became one of Faith's new pals. She helped fill the void in Faith's life. Also, they were both determined to do well in school. Leasa could be a lot of fun, but sometimes Faith wasn't so sure if they were always on the same page with choices.

"Hey, let's get our homework done after work and then go to a party," Leasa suggested.

"I don't know, Leasa." Faith hesitated. "My dad probably wouldn't like it if he knew I went to a party."

"You're kidding, right?" Leasa crossed her arms, and rolled her eyes as she let out a sigh. "How would your dad know?"

"Yeah, that's true." Faith felt guilty and stupid all at the same time. Guilty because lying to her dad is not something that Faith did. And stupid because she sometimes felt out of the loop with other teens her age. *I sure miss Robert. A lot.*

One evening as they left the grocery store, Leasa turned to Faith. "Why don't you tell your dad you're going to stay with me at my grandparents' house tonight? That way when we are done with our homework, we can go to that party, and he will never know how late you are out." Leasa always seemed to have things plotted out.

"Okay, but I want to go home first and grab my homework and some other clothes," Faith forced herself to say.

"I'll come with you," Leasa said.

Faith wondered if Leasa knew she was considering changing her mind about going out.

As they pulled into the driveway, Johnny and Mr. George were leaning the rake against the barn door. They met on the cement walk to the large farmhouse. Faith's dad smiled and bent over as he kissed Faith on the forehead, asking who her friend was.

"This is Leasa. I told you about her. We work together and see each other around school."

"Hi, Leasa." Mr. George held the door for both of the girls and Johnny.

As they entered the kitchen, Elisa wore an apron with a bright yellow sunflower design as she prepared dinner.

"Leasa, this is Elisa. I'll go grab my stuff and will be right back." Faith needed a few minutes alone.

As Elisa, Johnny, and Leasa stood in the kitchen, Johnny grabbed a piece of cornbread and exited the kitchen as fast as he could. Elisa tried to make small talk.

"Tell me about your family, Leasa." Elisa smiled.

"Not much to tell. I live with my grandparents." She snorted and glanced around at the kitchen.

"Do you like working at the grocery store?" Elisa smiled as though she didn't notice Leasa's rudeness.

"It will help me to get out of this town. That and doing well in school are my ticket out."

Just then, Faith came down the stairs. "Elisa, I'm going to do homework at Leasa's and stay the night. Would you tell Dad?"

"Did you ask him, honey?" Elisa was trying to soften the point she was making.

"No, but if he wants me to come home, will you just have him call me?" Faith offered.

Leasa headed for the door first.

"It was nice to meet you, Leasa," Elisa said.

"Thanks."

The girls hopped back into Leasa's car. Gravel flew from under the tires as the car raced down the driveway.

"Faith said she is staying the night at her new friend, Leasa's. She asked me to tell you." Elisa handed her husband the phone, then added, "She also said you can call her if you want her to come home."

"Why would I have her come home?" Mr. George pulled off one boot at a time as he sat at the table.

"Honey, I don't feel good about this." Elisa looked him in the eye, placing a chilled glass of whole milk in front of him.

"Elisa, I am glad that Faith has a new friend. I think she has been lonely. Anyway, I trust her." Faith's dad quickly emptied his glass.

In the next few months Leasa introduced Faith to parties and drinking. She also taught her how she was able to stay awake for hours and have endless energy. It began with caffeine pills, and then Leasa started buying little white pills from a guy who went to college she had met at a party.

A lot changed for Faith. Leasa was someone to hang out with while Robert was away at college, and Faith was meeting new friends, but her relationship with her family was becoming strained.

Faith couldn't figure out why Elisa didn't trust Leasa. She felt it every time Leasa came over. She was nice and all, but she asked more questions when they would go out, always telling them to be careful as they left the house.

"Careful of what?" Leasa snapped one Friday night with a growl in her voice. She slammed her door as they jumped in her car. "Your stepmom is a pain. Does she always have her Bible on the table? That would drive me nuts." Disgust filled the car.

"Not always." Faith wanted to defend Elisa. Though her stepmom had been reading her Bible a lot lately, ever since Trish, a friend from church, had given it to her. Faith honestly saw nothing annoying about it. She was more irritated that Leasa had been a jerk about Elisa.

The next day Faith headed for another week of classes. *If I can get through this week, I will get to see Robert. Man, I miss him.* Friday couldn't arrive fast enough.

When Friday rolled around, Robert called and said he would meet her at her house after she got home from school. But as she left her last class, juggling an armload of books, Robert sauntered up with a huge gleaming smile and a single red rose.

Erasing her shock, Robert embraced her. Onlookers stared, and Faith melted in his arms. When their hug ended, Robert looked at the girl he left behind and noticed how worn out she looked. It was Friday, after all, so he excused his concerns. He explained that he had to go home and see his parents. "I had to see you first," he whispered, then hugged her again.

Faith's heart burst, being reminded of how much she had missed him.

Early the next morning the sun couldn't rise soon enough. After she helped her father with chores, Robert was going to take her to lunch at their favorite burger place, like old times. She hated doing farm stuff now. Lately she didn't like being home much at all.

When Robert drove in, Johnny zipped out in front of Faith to meet him. As Faith came to the car, she shot a scowl Johnny's way. Didn't he know that Robert was there to see her? Robert didn't miss her agitation. Though Faith and Robert had been calling one another regularly, he wasn't aware of the significant changes that had happened since he had left.

There had also been many momentous changes in the George family. Robert would soon find out how Faith, as well as her family, had been transformed in differing significant ways.

"How is school going?" Robert asked as they both reached for the basket of fries. "Are you excited about going to college?"

"I'm excited about getting out of high school and out of the house. I don't think I'm going anywhere. I am probably gonna take classes at the community college and hopefully live with a friend." Faith's irritation hovered over the table.

"Well, that's all right. A lot of people transfer after two years." Robert tried to encourage her.

"Yeah, we'll see." Faith shrugged as her smile left her face. "How is school going for you?" Faith wanted to talk more about him than herself.

"I love it. I have gotten to meet some astounding, sharp friends, and my professors are incredible. It looks like I will get some leadership opportunities on campus. Someone even asked if I thought about being an officer for the freshman class."

Robert's living in a different world. "That is great," Faith said, trying to offer the enthusiasm he deserved.

"Faith, what's wrong?" Robert reached over and caressed her hand, unable to ignore or hide his concern anymore.

"It just seems like we're different now." Faith hung her head, thinking about her life and friends since Robert had been away.

"It won't be that way forever. Remember?" Robert gently put his hand behind Faith's head and pulled her close to him. He smiled, just inches away from her. Then he leaned over and gently kissed her forehead. She closed her eyes, wishing this moment would never end.

"Faith, how about if we hang out at your house on Sunday? I have missed your family," he asked as he pulled up to her home.

"That's fine with me, but since you've been away, they go to church now. Well, everyone except my dad. He sometimes stays home."

"Really?" Robert seemed shocked.

"Yeah, it is something Elisa has been doing. She takes the little kids with her."

"Do you ever go?" Robert wondered if this was a part of the distance he felt between them.

"Sometimes. You know, on special occasions. I will probably go to the Christmas Eve service. Elisa has already asked me. A lot of Saturday nights I hang out with Leasa, so I stay overnight at her house and come home when the others are at church."

"Yeah, you mentioned you had become friends with Leasa on the phone. What do you two do when you hang out?" Robert looked Faith in the eyes.

"We do homework." Faith said to soften the blow. "And then we usually go to a party."

"Really? What kind of party?" The weight of the question made her heart race.

"A party at a college dorm." Her feelings of shame filled her chest.

"Are you safe at those parties?" Robert's sudden honest question shocked Faith. And Robert. He had not planned to ask it. It just came out.

"Yes," she whispered and nodded. She stared at her frayed jeans.

Robert put his hand on her knee and gave it a gentle squeeze.

She looked at him and realized how much she had changed. Why did he have to leave her all alone? With no one but Leasa.

A tear started to trickle down her cheek. "It has been a really long week. I think I should go in." The hum of her phone in her pocket interrupted her thoughts. It was Leasa.

Robert sat there as they spoke.

"I can't tonight. I'm sorry, I thought I told you Robert was coming home."

Robert waited silently as Faith fidgeted with a hole in her jeans.

"I don't think he would be interested. I'll talk to you later in the week, and we will decide then. How does that sound?" Faith spoke in hushed tones as she glanced at Robert.

Faith took the phone from her ear and looked at it. Silence.

"Faith, what is going on?" Robert tried to swallow the lump of concern in his throat.

"I just need to go inside. I'm sorry."

Unstoppable Truth: Choices

Esther had some gut-wrenching, life-altering choices to make. Choices that would shake the foundations of history for her people, the Jews. In Esther 4:10–11 we saw Esther want to dash from those grim realities, burying her pretty little head in the sand. She either didn't believe how serious it was or didn't see the significance of the role she played in the drama her life was becoming. This is true of Faith too. It has also been true of me, and dear reader, maybe you too?

Divine providence will guide and demand each one of us to make choices that will bolster our emotional and spiritual health.

1. Please read Esther 4:15–5:14. I love God's reminders of how He leads. Esther's story is such a great example. "And who knows but that you have come to your royal position for such a time as this?" must have rung in her ears, rocking her soul.

   When our emotions are frayed and clarity is a mist that floats away, in those times we need to dig deep, both into our souls and into God's Word. That is where He can shape us to be the people He has called us to be—people of dignity, strength, and beauty. God will bring wisdom and clarity. He does that in various ways, often through a wise advisor who has the guts to tell us the truth we need to hear. Hard truth!

   - After being called out by Mordecai, what did Esther ask Mordecai to do (Esther 4:15–16)?
   - What promise did she make (verse 16)?

- What resolution did she make (verse 16)?
- What emotions do you think may have been going through Mordecai's head as he carried out Esther's, the girl he had raised, requests (verse 17)?

2. Look at Esther 5:1–4. Let's face it—this was a gutsy move. Esther had learned from her predecessor that integrity didn't always pay off. Sometimes integrity can put your pretty little head under the polished razorblade of a guillotine. Esther knew that.

- What difficult choice did Esther make? (I love this so much; it is such a triumphant picture of Esther's character being reinvigorated!)

This move was not about her. It was for a greater good than her own position. We will learn what it was truly about later. Her actions would have a historic impact. Folks, grab a cup of your favorite caffeinated beverage; I am going to take you on an insightful tour of what Esther was up against.

- People love to trace their family roots. They pay for kits, dispense spittle into a tube, and find out who their people were and are. Technology has opened the gates to jaw-dropping reports. Matthew 1:1–17 gives the genealogy of Esther and Mordecai, and this shows the importance of Mordecai's calling. Abraham was promised in Genesis 12:1–3 that all the generations would be blessed. That blessing was the coming of a Savior who would offer salvation to the world. After Abraham's uncommon show of faith, what did God promise him (Genesis 22:15–18)?

- What does God promise David in 2 Samuel 7:8–16?

- In Matthew 1:1–17 we see the lengthy genealogy of Jesus, the Messiah. In Matthew 1:2 we see Abraham highlighted, and in Matthew 1:6 David is listed. What does this verify?

- Matthew 1:2b says "Jacob the father of Judah and his brothers." One of those brothers is Benjamin (Genesis 35:16–18). As we read Esther 2:5, we see that Mordecai was a Benjamite (a descendant of Benjamin).

Satan threatened Christ's birth from the beginning of time. Satan's goal throughout history was to thwart God's promise of a coming Messiah to save us from our sins, thus bringing us into a right relationship with God. He (Satan) desired to make God a liar by destroying the opportunity for Christ, our Savior, to enter the scene.

He used Haman's evil decisions as his latest plot. If all Jews were destroyed, who would that include?

3. We already know that Mordecai is an amazing man of faith, but let's back up to Esther 4:13–14. What did he apparently understand about the will of God?

4. Look at Esther 5:5–9.
    - Why do you think Esther didn't just ask for what she desired at the first banquet?

- Waiting for God's leading and His perfect timing can be so hard at times, but He is a God of perfect timing. What happened in Esther 5:9–14 that was providential?
- What emotions did the evil Haman want Mordecai to feel? (We will discuss this later in the goal-setting section).

5. Faith had hard decisions to make as she faced various pressures. What were those pressures? She had godly allies as well. Who were they?

Reflection: You and I have to make choices like this every day. Providential choices that will impact us, our people, and maybe history. Decisions that God has placed before us. He desires that the outcome of what we decide will enhance our dignity, inner beauty, and ultimately, peace.

Chapter 9

Transformed

Echoes of laughter, raucous competitions in the field or at the game table, conversations of education, and spiritual discussions filled Sunday afternoons at the Georges home. Robert loved being a part of it. He was thrilled to reunite with Faith's kid brother, Johnny, and the little girls. Robert couldn't ignore the difference Elisa's presence brought to the family since the first time he had visited. It was tangible; peaceful and warm, more like his own. The distinct, colorful décor and dinner with all the fixings were also a transformation since he had been away at college. A lot had changed about this family, and Faith had changed in significant ways too.

Mr. George had come in from doing chores one evening and joined everyone around the dinner table.

"Faith, I like it when Robert is at our house." Betty's smile erupted, as her rosy cheeks scrunched in delight.

"Thanks, Bet." Robert was glad to be sitting around the table. He remembered how much this family meant to him. "I like coming to see you!" Robert put his hand up, offering a high-five, something he had taught this little tot before he left for college.

She lowered her hand before Robert could tap it. "Missed me." Betty giggled.

"Oh, boy—you've gotten quick since I was gone! You tricked me."

"I know. Do you want to see me wun when we play tag? I'm the fastest!" Betty always thought Robert came to visit her.

"Betty, you can play outside later. We want to hear about Robert's college." Elisa smiled at Betty, who put her hands on her lap and sucked her dimpled cheek as she prepared for a long sit.

As the family sat around the table, Robert told them about his classes. He loved his professors and how much they taught him. He had gotten involved in clubs that showed off his academics and his leadership skills. He especially enjoyed French Club and his Marketing and International Business course. Robert also told Faith's family he was considering traveling abroad. His excitement beamed when he talked about the opportunities. His advisor had hand-picked him for an internship with an American company with a division in France.

"Cool," Johnny said.

"Yeah, I also was elected president of the French Club, so when the chance came up, I applied and was accepted."

Faith sat silently, turning away from Robert with a pained

expression.

"That is wonderful, Robert." Elisa smiled at him, then glanced at Faith. She couldn't help but notice that Faith had a blank look on her face.

"I don't know if I'll go. There's a lot of money to raise, and I would be away for a whole semester." Robert glanced at Faith, who was now staring at her plate, her slumped shoulders looking as if she wanted to slither under the table.

"Sounds amazing, man." Johnny seemed shocked that Robert was even questioning accepting this option.

"Congratulations, young man," Faith's dad said. "Sounds like you're making the most of college and this prospect."

"Thank you, Mr. George. I'm sure trying," Robert knew that compliments from Mr. George were not handed out often.

"Robert and Faith, why don't you kids go for a walk?" Elisa tilted her head at Mr. George and then made eye contact with each of Faith's siblings, "We can clean up."

"I wanna go." Betty scrunched her eyes at Robert, lifting her arms toward him.

"No, you stay here. We're going to have ice cream with sprinkles," Elisa said, enticing her.

"Okay, I go yater with Wobert and Faith." Betty nodded, trying to convince Elisa.

"Thank you, ma'am." Robert stood and pulled out Faith's chair.

As the leaves crunched under her feet and the breeze carried the sweet smell of autumn, Robert grasped Faith's hand. "I'm sorry. I should have told you earlier,"

"It's Okay." Faith kept her head bowed and her shoulders slumped.

"It's going to help in our future," Robert tried to explain.

"I know." Faith had so many thoughts running through her mind and could say only those couple of words. She wondered if they had a future, knowing they were moving away from each other. Did he feel it too?

Robert's tender grip emphasized the shame Faith was trying to submerge. How could she tell him about the parties and the people she had been hanging out with since he had gone away to college? In his presence she felt safe and warm. And confused and scared. She needed to stop hanging out with Leasa. It would be tough, but she needed to.

"Faith, did you hear me?" Robert wrapped his arms around her.

"I'm sorry, Robert. What did you say?" She looked up into his safe blue eyes.

"Let's go get some of that ice cream." His gleaming smile reminded her of their first date.

"It won't be forever, Faith. One day all these adventures will be ours . . . together." Robert kissed her on the forehead before they turned back to the house.

It didn't take long for Robert to become the class president. He traveled to France and worked there for one semester. Faith couldn't shake Leasa and found herself in her grip. The differences between Faith and Robert were becoming as wide as the Grand Canyon, but something kept them dreaming about their future together.

Home had changed too.

"Hi, sweet girl." Elisa glanced up from her Bible that sat next to her cup of decaf coffee on the dining room table. "You heading out this evening?"

"To see Robert. He just got home from college." Faith's tone was subdued.

"Wonderful. I can't believe he will be done in one semester." Elisa was nudging a gentle reminder to her stepdaughter.

"Yeah, me neither." Faith bit her bottom lip, as she took in small rhythmic breaths.

"Do you kids have any plans?" Elisa knew she was taking a risk with this question. "For the future?"

"I don't know," Faith whispered. Her shoulders drooped as she reached across the table to grab a roll from dinner.

"Faith, is there anything you want to talk about?" Elisa smiled and leaned her chin on her clasped hands. Her heart was broken over the changes Faith thought she was hiding from the family.

Faith shook her head and swept an unexpected tear from her cheek.

"If you ever want to talk, I'm here." Elisa looked her in the eyes and reached out for her hand.

"Thank you. I know." Faith felt the safety of being in Elisa's presence. As she went to face Robert, she glanced back at Elisa, who had gone back to her reading.

The tears continued to trickle down Faith's face as she sat across from Robert at their favorite restaurant. Robert had led them to the back table where no one else was seated.

"I just feel distant from you. I don't get it. But honestly, I have felt this way for a while." Robert's brows drew together as his hand stroked the nape of his neck.

"I know." Faith let out a sigh of relief as she shook her head, knowing it was time to tell him everything.

"What's up?" Robert kept his hands on his lap as his blue eyes pierced her own.

"I've just changed. It was hard when you were away." She had to be honest with him.

"It was hard for me too." His voice was firm.

"I made it even harder." Her voice trailed off as she thought about the last few months. She hung her head as she clasped her hands between her knees.

"Faith, I think we need to give each other time." Robert looked away.

Afterward, Elisa didn't ask a lot of questions, but Faith knew she must have picked up on the fact that Robert had broken up with her. Faith was grateful she never said anything.

After her last talk with Robert at the restaurant, Faith harnessed the courage to end her friendship with Leasa. One day she simply wrote Leasa a note, saying she was feeling really guilty about the parties and choices she had made and that she wouldn't be doing that stuff anymore. It was one of the hardest things she had ever done. She left it in Leasa's locker at work. That afternoon Faith heard Leasa and her coworkers joking about her at work as Leasa read the note she had written out loud to them. Faith didn't care anymore.

On the first weekend that Faith had not made plans with Leasa, Elisa tapped on Faith's bedroom door. She came in and sat next to Faith on her bed. With a tender smile that told Faith she understood, she looked into Faith's eyes. "Tomorrow morning we thought we would go to lunch after church. Do you want to join us? You can pick the restaurant."

"Sure," Faith whispered with a gentle nod. "That sounds fine."

"I'll let your dad know." As Elisa stood, she bent over and wrapped her arms around Faith. "I love you so much." Her stepmother whispered the words Faith had ached to hear.

Tears welled in Faith's eyes. "I know you do" was all she could get out.

At church the pastor spoke about trusting God. *He must know what's going on in my life.*

He told the story of Mary, the mother of Jesus, and the position she found herself in when she was pregnant with Jesus. "How must she have felt? This was not her decision; it was decided for her. It was part of a magnificent plan."

Faith felt that she could relate a little to Mary and decisions being made by another person that would alter her life. One thing Faith couldn't ignore was how her own lousy choices had gotten her to this place. She had never heard a sermon that made her feel this way before—that she wanted to be different.

As the pastor was wrapping up, it was as if he were reading Faith's mind. "When we can't understand what is going on, we can do one thing. Trust in the Lord." Then he paused for what seemed like five minutes, looking around at the congregation. "Lean not on your own understanding." The room was silent.

Faith looked at her big strong dad, who nodded. He put his arm around Elisa and pulled her close.

"In all your ways acknowledge Him, meaning give Him control."

"Amen," Elisa whispered.

"And he will direct your path. He promises that, folks. He will direct you when you just don't know what to do." At that moment Faith was so glad she had come. She wasn't sure why or what this meant in her life, but she had a calm in her heart she couldn't remember ever feeling before. As the large George family exited the church, the young pastor shook each person's hand. He looked Faith in the eye and smiled. "I'm so glad you came today, young lady."

"Me too." Faith felt a peace come over her.

"Where are we going to lunch, Faith?" Dad asked as everyone got into the van after church.

"Can we go to the hamburger place in town?" The family didn't know it was because Faith had missed her time there with Robert.

"Sure," Elisa said. "We said it was your choice."

As the family sat in a booth, the younger kids were chattering about their church classes and what they had learned. Elisa prayed before the food arrived at the table and thanked God for His provisions, for Faith being with them, and for the reminder to trust God. When the waitress brought their meals, the chattering ended for a few moments as the hungry family enjoyed their meals.

"I felt like the pastor had read my mail." Faith broke the silence.

"I feel like that every Sunday." Dad smiled at Elisa, taking a sip of his water.

"You do?" Faith was shocked by her dad's openness.

"Yup." He took a bite of his burger.

As they finished and headed toward the door, Elisa wrapped her arm around Faith's shoulders. "Faith, I have to go shopping. Want to join me? I thought we could grab some stuff for your graduation party."

"Sure."

As they got home from the restaurant, the two of them exited the van and got into Elisa's car.

"Have you thought about who you are inviting?" Elisa asked as she backed away from the house.

"I haven't." Faith's answer was honest and hollow.

For the last four months Faith hadn't heard a peep from Robert. She wished she could tell him how she had changed. Her heart ached as she thought about him. She surprised herself by graduating eleventh in her class, just missing the opportunity for accolades and many scholarships. Putting the brakes on the time she spent with Leasa helped. She also stopped making other choices that only led to deep regret.

Preparing for graduation had been difficult. Hearing other classmates talk about their graduation plans with their families made her think about her mother. And Robert. She couldn't change that they were not in her life, but for the first time, she decided she could allow herself to hurt. She hurt for her losses, but she also yearned to have everything she had thrown away.

"I'd love to help you write invitations if you'd like," Elisa offered.

"Thanks." *Elisa is about the only friend I have left.* That truth stung her heart. "I have thought about sending an invitation to Robert, but I don't know. What do you think?" She really wanted Elisa's opinion.

"That is a sweet idea. Do you think he would come?" Elisa had never brought his name up, but she must have known what had happened.

"I don't know." Faith's eyes were vacant.

"Maybe you should call him first and ask." Elisa's hard-hitting request prompted the courage Faith needed.

They pulled up to the house and she made the call. As the

phone rang, Faith's stomach flipped upside down. *I hope this is a good idea.*

"Faith?" She could hear Robert's shock.

"Hi." Her heart jumped into her throat.

"Hey—what're you up to?" Robert's smile penetrated the phone. "Aren't you graduating soon?"

"I graduate in two weeks."

"Wow—that's awesome." He sounded sincerely excited.

"I wondered . . ." Faith stood in her front yard, the only quiet place around while looking at her empty driveway. "I wondered if you could make it to my party."

"Sure," he said quietly. "I can do that."

"I'll send you an invitation and see you then." Faith's heart beat quickly.

"Sounds great." Robert's kind voice hadn't changed.

Elisa and Faith's dad put together a wonderful graduation celebration. With appetizers, punch, and cake, it was different from some of the other parties going on that day. It was exactly what Faith wanted.

Faith stood at the front door, thanking the extended family who had come when she saw Robert pull up. He climbed out. *He is still so handsome.*

"Hi." His smile brought back a flood of emotions that Faith quickly shoved down.

"Hi. Thanks for coming. Come in."

Just as she said that, Robert heard the familiar welcome he had missed.

"Hey, man. Glad you're here. Throw the football later?" Johnny now towered over Robert and displayed a genuine smile.

Betty gave him a special welcome, "Where you at, Robert?"

"Where have you been?" Her father corrected her, tossling her golden curls.

Scooping her up in his arms, Robert spun her in a circle. "I've been missing you. That is where I've been."

"I have been missing you too." Betty laid her blonde locks on his shoulder.

Elisa appeared by Robert's side. "It is nice to see you, young man. Please come in. The rest of the guests are just gathering their coats, so it's the perfect time to catch up."

"Welcome." Mr. George glanced at Faith, wishing he could see her heart, as he shook Robert's hand.

Sitting around the table, Robert asked Faith where she planned on going to college. She told him of her plans to go to the two-year college in town. Though she didn't have a specific program she wanted to study, she knew she wanted to do something that helped people.

"I think I would do a great job with children or teenagers. Probably counseling or something like that."

"You would be great at that," Robert said. "You have always been great with people."

"Yeah, maybe something to help families who have struggled with alcoholism." Faith glanced at her father.

"That may be your calling, dear." Elisa gathered the cups from the table and smiled at Faith.

"Yup, sure would. Especially if you can make money doing it," Dad added.

As Robert got up to leave later, Faith walked him to the door. He bent down and gave her one of the hugs she had missed so much.

"Thank you for coming," she whispered in his ear. "I'm sorry for everything."

He put his gentle hands on her shoulders and looked into her beautiful eyes—the eyes he had fallen in love with years ago. "Can you walk me out to my car?"

As they got near his car, Robert took Faith's hand. "Beautiful Faith, I have thought about you every day. Can we talk?"

"Sure, but it's late and getting chilly." Faith wrapped her sweater tightly around her waist. "Can we sit in your car?"

Robert opened her door just as he had the first time years ago. The memories of how much they had cared for one another came flooding back into her heart.

Faith relived the last year for Robert that night. As the moon brightened the sky and the stars twinkled cheerfully, she told him things he already knew, like how lonely she was when he was away. She told him about having to make new friends because when he left there was a big hole in her life. Then she told him many things he didn't know. She told him about Leasa, parties, drugs, and losing sight of what was important, like family and those who love her.

Robert reached around her shoulders and pulled her close. "Was there ever anyone else, Faith?" His reasonable question made tears fall from her lashes.

"Never," she assured him. "Never."

He kissed her on the forehead. "Faith, I want you to marry me." He kissed her wet cheek.

"I need to go to college, and you have so much going on in your life." Faith felt that she was seeing life more clearly than ever before.

"We can both do those things. But we can do them together. I don't want to be apart anymore. These last few months killed me. I hated not seeing or talking to you. I thought maybe there was someone else." Robert realized how much he loved and needed Faith.

"It's always just been you."

They were both silent for a few seconds.

"Yes, I will marry you," she said. "I don't want to be apart either."

In the coming months the couple began making plans. After Faith graduated from high school, they would move to Seattle, where Robert had already accepted a job offer.

"Faith and Robert," Elisa said after a Sunday dinner while they were clearing the table, "I wondered if you would consider speaking to our pastor about your upcoming marriage and wedding."

Faith looked at Robert. They both knew the impact that the pastor and the church had on Elisa and the family. Elisa confided once to Faith that she and her dad had gone to speak with their pastor about their marriage and blending their families. Faith could see that their relationship had changed. They all went to church on Sundays and Johnny was even involved in a Bible study. Robert saw the difference too, but he knew this would be a challenge for his family to swallow.

Robert was expected to marry in the church that his parents attended when they were married, and their parents before them. Robert considered it his church also since his family attended on Easter and Christmas every year.

Faith told Robert about how much she was learning from the sermons when she had gone to church with the family. Though

Robert didn't care what church they married in, he knew it mattered to his family. He agreed to meet with the pastor at the church that the George family had been attending.

"Regardless of where you have your ceremony, I would be happy to do some premarital counseling," the young minister, who was dressed in jeans and a black T-shirt, offered. "I just want to give you some things to think about to assure your success in marriage. It would be my wedding gift to you." He smiled, looking at each one from behind his desk.

"Sure, pastor." Robert looked at Faith as if asking if it were Okay with her.

Faith smiled, nodding at her handsome fiancé.

"Just call me Nick." The minister stood and shook each of their hands.

Unstoppable Truth: Transformed

"Show me who your five closest friends are, and I will know you." The young youth minister preached the same words I heard uttered in my youth. Proven truths. Friendships can make or break us, so choose carefully who you want to be. Haman seemed to surround himself with like-minded people. Be warned: we all do.

In this Bible study and in the "Setting Your Own Goals" section at the end of the book, I will unearth some truths that will help you make positive, enduring relationships. I will also provide some needful guardrails to keep you from the ditch of dangerous liaisons.

1. Please read Esther 5:14 again. What did Haman's closest confidant and his friends advise him to do?
   - Really look at that verse. After preparing to have someone killed, what did they tell him to do at the banquet? (Yikes!)

We are who we choose to hang around. This is a biblical truth, and it is a truth we all have understood since we were in junior high or middle school. But even as adults we have to be cautious about choosing our tribe.

The story that follows is a present-day true example of a dear friend and her son.

Side-by-side, we had snuggled our little ones in the church rockers, laughing, cooing, and dreaming. Then life happened. My close confidant and her husband had jobs that required some Sunday shifts. Their kids were also involved on elite sports teams, which meant they missed many Wednesday and Sunday church services. Soon they purchased a new home in the next town over, making the commute too difficult. And the kids other activities gobbled up their schedule. Eventually my friend and her family dropped off the face of the planet.

It wasn't until the shockwaves hit our community—a violent murder committed by three youths—that we realized they were still out there. But everything had changed. What happened to that sweet little bundle who had been sung "Jesus Loves Me" at the breast of his mother, my close friend? He and his friends had conspired in a robbery that escalated to murder.

Bad company corrupts good character. It's always true! For kids, and for you and me. My dear friend's broken heart tells the story, as does Proverbs.

2. Please read Proverbs 1:10–19.

   I honestly don't know who instigated the murder. But I do know that that sweet little guy I knew and his co-defendants are behind bars. And I have to face the fact that the once-precious toddler had choices he made all along the way.

   - In Proverbs 1:10 what is the first response any of us can make when enticed?
   - What is the lure (verses 11–14)?
   - What strong advice are we all given (verse 15)?

- What outcome can we be assured of (verses 16–19)? And this is exactly the plight of my dear friend's son.

3. Now let's talk about you and me. This drama also plays out in those church rockers, pews, and homes of folks like you and me.

   When my first little cherub was born, I had just moved three thousand miles away from everyone I loved and the godly people who had mentored me. After walking into my new church, I immediately had a small group of friends. I was accepted.

   At nap time I would lay my angel in his crib, and for the next three hours I would cling to my phone talking to my new friends. At first they would tell me about themselves, and then they started to tell me about everyone else in the church. I felt filthy and filled with guilt as I listened. I frittered away the only quiet moments I had to get rest myself and do things like wash bottles and get the small apartment we were living in cleaned up. Until one day I realized that the choice of how I spent my time belonged to me and me alone.

> *"Work willingly at whatever you do,*
> *as though you were working for*
> *the Lord rather than for people"*
> (Colossians 3:23 NLT)

- Please read 1 Corinthians 15:58. What are we instructed to do?
- Please read Psalm 39:4. What are we reminded about our days?

Amid diapers, meal prep, church events, concerts, and sports, the days can seem so long, but when we look back, those years were so very short. They truly fly by. We will never be able to recapture wasted moments.

- In what areas of your life could you be using your time more effectively?
- I needed to be reminded of the truths I knew about friendships. Please read Ephesians 4:29, as I did, and let's dig out the nuggets that will guide us to God-honoring relationships.
- What is the first directive given in that verse?
- What do our words need to be used for?
- What should be the point of our speech?

That was not happening as that sweet baby slept. It didn't take long for me to begin to feel really guilty. I felt as if I needed a shower after some of those conversations, and it was back in the day when phone cords stretched only so far (Google search "vintage phone cord"). So when I had stretched the cord far enough to do the dishes or organize the bookshelf, then I was stuck absorbing all the negative gossip. I knew I was wasting time. And sinning.

4. So what could I do? I will give you a hint. Even though I knew how to do right, I was sometimes a coward back then. Thankfully, I was in the Word and I knew what I should do. The hints to what I did are found in the following verses.

   - Proverbs 14:1
   - Titus 2:3–5
   - 1 Timothy 5:14
   - Psalm 32:7

   You got it. I hid. I stopped answering the phone in the afternoon. This is back when those phones with long cords didn't let you know who was calling, so I had to tell my mother, mother-in-law, and husband that I wasn't answering the phone during naptime anymore. This lasted about two weeks before each lady cornered me at church and asked where I was in the afternoon. I told them the truth—that I was doing my chores and taking a nap sometimes. I left out the part about avoiding a soul shower. Eventually our friendships simmered to the point that I was no longer involved in unhealthy conversations.

5. One of the most life-giving verses God placed in my hands and heart is 2 Corinthians 5:17. Please write it out in the space below.

   Because God is creating us new, just as He was doing in Elisa and Mr. George, what should some of our new choices look like? Specifically, what choices will you make regarding your time or friendships as a result of the verses you read in this section?

I love this truth from Philippians 1:6 (NABRE): "I am confident of this, that the one who began a good work in you will continue to complete it until the day of Christ Jesus."

God is doing the work, and He isn't done with me! That gives me peace! He will continue to change and transform me and you if we will let Him. Will you? Below, make a prayerful commitment to God to change something that you hear Him impressing on your heart. Date it so you can look back and see His work in your life over the years.

Dear Lord,

_____
_____
_____
_____
_____
_____
_____
_____
_____

Chapter 10

Shattered

The tenacious, grind-it-out effort paid off for Robert. He was determined to be the best, and he succeeded. He hit all his sales goals in the first six years of their marriage. They were living the dream they had prepared for.

As their bank account grew, their family grew as well. Robert's business success afforded Faith the luxury to stay home and nurture their three children. Her devoted personality also provided Robert with the opportunity to shine. Faith's college aspirations were replaced with Robert's ambitions to succeed. His accomplishments were her only goal. Bringing her along to corporate festivities always bode well for Robert as Faith's infectious admiration for him bolstered respect from his colleagues.

Robert also appreciated everything she did to raise their children. Eventually, though, her responsibilities at home and helping at the kid's school kept her from joining Robert on many trips. As they busied themselves at home and Robert traveled 300 days a year, Robert began to feel disconnected from his family. He consoled himself by believing that this was the cost of the corporate life, which he had desired.

Faith also felt that they were drifting apart. She often didn't know where he planned to travel to next, but she did know he was doing what he loved, achieving success. With each parting, it seemed that his absence broadened the abyss between them. Faith also told herself that this was just part of corporate life.

With ten years and multiple company awards on Robert's résumé, the young man Faith had fallen in love with had become unrecognizable.

"Hi, hun," Faith said when she finally got a hold of him one day. She was happy to hear his voice after trying to call him for two days with no answer.

"Did you need something, Faith? I'm swamped."

"I just wanted to tell you about the kids' day." Faith felt the excitement leave her heart like the air from a pin-pricked balloon.

"I'm so busy. I really can't talk now. Can it wait till this weekend?" Robert whispered.

Faith could hear what sounded like a party in the background. "Where are you?" Faith wondered how his trip to Dallas was going.

"What do you mean? You know I told you I was meeting with clients in New York all week."

"You told me that you were traveling to Dallas for a planning meeting with your boss," Faith reminded him.

Robert paused. "Oh, yeah—on my way to the airport I got a call from corporate. They needed me here instead." Laughter in the background competed with Robert's voice. "Faith, I need to go." Robert ended the call.

Faith fumbled to get the kids' pajamas ready. Running up the steps to their rooms, she felt her heart tighten as she thought of Robert. He was usually busy, but tonight he was obviously put off by her call.

Faith reached for her phone numerous times in the next couple of days. She wanted Robert to give her a good explanation for their last bizarre conversation. But she set the phone down each time, knowing she needed to wait until they were alone and face to face.

"Hi, hun," Robert said as he walked through the solid oak doors. He set his briefcase down in the expansive foyer.

Drawings that his children made greeted him. "Welcome home, Dad."

He spotted a big red heart that Faith must have made that said, "I LOVE YOU!"

Faith watched from the kitchen as he paused to read each one. His shoulders dropped as he rubbed the back of his neck.

The kids charged toward him.

"Daddy, Daddy, Daddy, we missed you." Seven-year-old Maddison, with her pigtails flying, wrapped her arms around his knees.

"Dad, wanna play catch today and watch the game?" said four-year-old Peter. He jumped over the back of the couch and leaped into Robert's arms.

"Did you get a haircut?" asked six-year-old Sadie. "That looks funny. Dad, oh, your hair looks like that guy on those Bachelor commercials." She wrinkled her freckled nose and narrowed her eyes.

Faith thought the same thing. "Hi, hun. New shirt and shoes?" She was surprised at how casual Robert looked coming home from a business trip.

"Yeah, I had some time, so I did a little shopping." Robert shoved his hands deep into his pockets as his shoulders tightened.

"We can play ball and watch the game." Robert swooped Peter into a cradle motion. Bending in half, he kissed Sadie.

Sadie tapped the top of his head. "Dad, your hair feels funny. Like a porcupine. It's stiff on top." Her eyes narrowed.

"It's gel. Leave it be."

"You look like one of the boys at the mall." Sadie crossed her arms, then rolled her eyes.

"Children, your dad looks handsome. Be nice." Faith leaned toward Robert for a kiss and he met her with a quick peck.

"Thanks, Faith." He glanced away from her smile.

The next day as they huddled in the living room, the children were piled next to Robert on the couch.

"Mom, come sit with us," Maddison said. "We'll make room. Dad, will you scoot over for Mom, please?"

Robert hesitated, grabbed the blanket that covered him, and without taking his eyes off the game on TV, he made a small space on the couch.

"Thank you, Maddison. I'm keeping an eye on supper, so I'll sit here." Faith tried to hide a tear as she watched Robert with the kids.

Robert grabbed the football after dinner and raced around the yard with his homemade team. Faith sighed, watching from the kitchen window at what a devoted father he was.

After tucking the little ones in, Faith told Robert about a church in town that two of her friends attended. She wondered if he wanted to take the kids.

"I have some plans to finalize before I travel next week. Why don't you take them?"

She reached for Robert's laundry. "Here—I can add those to the load I have."

He looked away. "I've got it; you're already busy enough."

Faith wondered if she had made Robert feel that she was too occupied with the kids, leaving him out in the cold. She would work on that.

At the height of his career Robert often asked Faith to travel with him. He was one of the top salespeople in the company. Faith often felt that on these trips she was the accessory he needed to complete the picture he was hoping to create.

On one particular weekend he was honored for making the company a lucrative international deal that would open his department up to new markets. This is the kind of respect Robert had dreamed of. Faith did not let him down. She showed up and stood by his side.

Laughter filled the table as Faith told stories of Robert and the children as they chose their fantasy football picks. Faith glanced around the table as the suits of the company replaced their stiff shirts for relaxed shoulders and echoing hilarity. Faith grinned and nodded at Robert, whose smile topped off the black suit and red tie she had laid out for him that evening.

The waitstaff refreshed the wine glasses throughout the night. Faith left her tonic water unattended. The sensual jazz music playing in the background echoed the emotion of the room.

"Robert, I think I better head up to our room soon," Faith whispered in his ear as they glided across the dance floor. Exhausted after preparing the kids for the weekend, packing, and racing to the airport, she knew the next day would be just as exhausting on the golf course. Entertaining Robert's team was a feat.

"Really?" His eyebrows turned inward and his shoulders widened as he looked down at her.

"I need to get some rest."

Robert ignored the dark circles under her eyes. "Okay, I'll be up in a bit."

Faith hobbled over to the elevator, and with a heavy sigh she nudged the button to take her up to their room. Stomping her ruby-red heels, she remembered that the key to her room was in her purse and both were under the table where she had been sitting. She scooted back to gather her things.

The dark room made focusing difficult, but one thing her eyes could not miss was that apparently the VIPs had gone to their rooms as well. And it was hard to miss how close Robert was sitting to the cute young girl on his sales team. She had been located across from him at the table. With a steely stare, Faith's tight lips whispered to Robert, "Excuse me—my purse is under that seat." He grimaced, then recovered quickly by making up a lame story about speaking to her about their next big deal.

The golden-haired, petite colleague blushed and stammered as she rummaged under the chair. "Uh, here it is." She pulled it out like a five-year-old handing her mother a flower from the garden.

Faith grabbed her purse and held back tears, then made a beeline to the elevator. Faith wept for fifteen floors, chiding herself for being so blind and stupid. *How did I not know?* She blamed herself.

Faith's life would never be the same.

As she undressed in the bathroom, she stared at the figure that had carried three children. For the first time she didn't like what she saw. As she brushed her hair, she asked herself why she had chopped it off years ago. Raising kids took a lot of time, and styling hair had gotten in the way, she reminded herself. As she put on her comfy cotton nightgown, she wondered if she should have brought the red silk nighty Robert had bought her for Christmas last year.

What am I going to do? That thought ran through her mind repeatedly into the wee hours of the morning until Robert finally crawled into the king-size bed, staying on the edge. Faith felt the ocean between them.

When Faith got home she replayed what she saw at the table that night. Sadly, she also replayed all the ways she had let herself go. She blamed herself. When she brought it up to Robert, at first he told her she was silly. When she adamantly disagreed, he raised his tone and told her she was ridiculous and jealous. Faith had never been jealous a day in her life. When she reminded Robert of what she saw at the table, he told her she had a great imagination. They rehashed this conversation over and over.

In the following weeks Faith changed her gym routine. Instead of going three days a week, she hit the machines at the gym five days a week for a couple of hours, convincing herself that she would dedicate her time and body to saving her marriage.

Being baffled by Faith's new ultra-intense passion, Tawana, a friend from church and the gym, put herself between Faith and the childcare door before she picked up her children. "What's up, girl?" She smiled, noticing Faith's bright red face and drips falling from her long bangs.

Faith's heart pounded and she gasped. "I can't talk . . . about it . . . right now." She forced back a tear. "I've let myself go." Faith shook her head.

"What?" Tawana couldn't believe those words came from Faith's mouth. "You look fine, honey." Tawana shook her head and grabbed Faith's shoulders, making her stare straight into her eyes. "Girlfriend, you're beautiful."

Debbie, another friend from the gym, panted and guzzled water nearby. "I could not keep up with you, lady. What is going on?" Feeling the heaviness in the small cluster, she looked at Tawana.

Faith nervously looked at her torso. "I'm a mess. I've let myself go, and when I got on the scale after our last trip . . ." Faith wiped tears from her eyes. "I just need to make my time at the gym work for me."

"Whatever." Debbie said. "All our scales are liars. You need to shut that thing up. Bring it over to my house and I'll have Bill introduce it to his sledgehammer." Debbie could usually make her gym pals laugh. But not today.

"Debbie is right." Tawana reached her arms around her hurting friend while smiling over her shoulder at Debbie as if to caution her. "None of us like what our scales say at times, but you look hot, honey." Tawana's dark brown eyes locked with Faith's as she tightened her tender arms around her. As she felt the comfort of her friend, the tears she had been holding back flowed.

Debbie stretched her arms around both, hoping their cluster would squeeze out the lies Faith was telling herself.

"Girl, come in here and tell us what is going on." Tawana opened the door of an empty room. The three of them unfolded metal chairs and sat in a circle. Faith told them that it didn't go well the last time they had traveled together. She relived Robert's weird behavior at home also, saying he had recently begun to comment on Faith's additional weight. He said he felt it had become an issue in their marriage. She confessed that she was feeling insecure with Robert for the first time in their lives.

"Sorry, girl, but . . ." Debbie anchored both hands on her hips and paused. "Robert is being a jerk. It's not you!"

Faith hated that Debbie felt that way. She also was grateful that someone put a word to how she was feeling. Yet she was still too embarrassed to tell them about the dinner. What if she was wrong? She really didn't want Robert to look bad. These were good friends. What would they think if they knew how chummy he was with his colleague? And what if Faith just misunderstood? What if she really did have a vivid imagination?

The image of the stunning professional at the table haunted Faith. Convinced that she was traveling on the same business trips that were keeping Robert so busy sent her mind down dark tunnels. Robert had denied it, but Faith saw it with her own eyes.

Faith's heart was splitting right down the middle. How could this be happening? She wouldn't tell Tawana and Debbie about the woman in case Robert was telling her the truth and her emotions were lying to her.

In the following weeks Tawana and Debbie continued to try to be there for Faith.

"Hey, Faith—want to go grab a salad after our workout?" Tawana asked as they entered spin class.

"I have to run to the school to help with a party." Faith always had a reason to decline. She couldn't bring herself to tell them anymore. She didn't want to believe it, and giving it words would only make it even more real.

A month of keeping it in the deepest part of her heart and turning it over repeatedly only brought more sadness. She needed to confide in someone. While putting each of her children in their Sunday school classes, she whispered to Tawana, "Can you come over after church today? I need to talk to someone."

"Debbie and I were going to go to lunch. Do you want to join us? Ebony, my oldest, can watch our little ones." Tawana smiled and wrapped an arm around Faith's shoulders.

"That would be all right."

It didn't surprise her two confidants as Faith began describing her marriage. Tears started to flow from each. Then Faith sat up, lifted her shoulders, and taking in a deep breath, told them both about what had happened when she had traveled with Robert. As she sucked in all the air from the room, she shared what her gut was telling her. She also told them Robert had convinced her it was nothing.

"Nothing?" Debbie sputtered. "What is nothing about this? This is something. That man!"

Faith wondered if she had said too much. She wasn't ready for her friends to interject advice.

Debbie had strong opinions and an even stronger sense of loyalty. She saw Faith as the most upbeat of them all, and now she was downcast, heartbroken, and in disbelief. "Faith, this isn't your fault, and it has nothing to do with how you think you look. This is on Robert."

"She's right," Tawana said. "This is not on you, sweetie. This *is* on Robert." She reached over and squeezed Faith's hand.

Faith now had the level of support she had always offered to everyone else. Moving to Seattle had been an opportunity for a fresh start for Faith's spiritual life. She wanted what Elisa and her father had. Attending church, she began reading the Bible also. Peace filled her soul in those quiet moments as she reflected on the words. The lessons the children retold from the backseat also taught Faith so many truths. Hoping Robert would feel the same, she often tried to convince him to join them. Usually he was too busy or didn't want to miss a game on TV.

Faith had also begun to attend a Bible study. One evening she asked to talk to the leader alone. She explained what had been going on in her marriage and confided that she knew her husband was having an affair. She was trying everything to save their marriage, but she said things were beginning to unravel. Sometimes she had no idea where Robert was for several days in a row. The leader just listened and tried to hear what she needed.

Faith wondered if her once-blissful marriage and family would ever be right again.

Robert had made a real mess of things. His continual lies and ongoing affair eventually became crystal clear. He no longer denied it or excused it. He had become his own god. The young man she fell in love with in high school no longer existed.

Faith had read a quote recently by a Christian author and speaker and it hit the nail on the head: "Sin will take you farther than you want to go, keep you longer than you want to stay, and cost you more than you want to pay."

Faith called her Bible study leader one Saturday morning. "I got a phone call from Robert last night. I am so frustrated and so scared for him."

"What happened?" Jennifer asked her.

"Robert called me after two in the morning. He told me someone had stolen his car. He was in the city, hanging out with some friends after work, and when he went to leave, his car was gone."

"Oh, my." The trusted guide was shocked that Robert's choices had spiraled so quickly that he was in such a predicament.

"So at 2:30 in the morning, I put the children in the car and went and got him." Faith's voice crumbled.

"You did what?" Jennifer yelped without thinking.

"I know! That's why I am calling you. Do you think I should do this for him if it happens again? I don't want to be an ungodly wife, but it was scary." Faith's voice quivered through the phone and reached across town.

"You know, I think that one of the pastors at the church should give you some input on this," Jennifer firmly advised.

"I don't want to call," she whispered and started to weep. "Would you call for me?"

Her spiritual guide consoled her, promising, "I will call you right back." For Faith's privacy, Jennifer avoided the receptionist and called the counseling pastor's office phone.

"Faith drove her kids into the drug-infested part of the city in the middle of the night," she told Jack. "I am calling you because Faith is afraid she will be looked at as unsubmissive if she tells Robert she doesn't feel comfortable doing that again. But I don't think Faith has any business being in that part of town with her little ones. What do you think?"

"You are right," Jack said. "Please tell Faith she doesn't need to do that if it happens again. Robert can take a rideshare or cab."

The counselor wasn't even sure if a rideshare or cab driver would go into that part of town, where murders were rampant, rapes were excessive, and thugs sold drugs like candy, especially at that hour.

"Also," Jack added, "please tell Faith and Robert that I am available to meet with them if I can help in any way."

"Thank you. I will."

She called Faith back. "Faith, you don't have to do that again. Robert's choices are not a submission issue. His decisions should not put you and your children in an unsafe environment unnecessarily. Jack said you're welcome to stop by with or without Robert. He's a great counselor. I would take him up on it."

Robert had no desire to meet with Jack or anyone else from the church, so Faith began meeting with Jack every week. In the first meeting Jack informed Faith that he had asked a police officer in their congregation about cars that had been stolen in that part of town without divulging any information about Robert and Faith.

"The most common illegal activity with cars in that part of town is 'users' trading them for drugs," the street cop had informed Jack.

As Jack relayed this to Faith, he also told her he wanted her to pray fervently not just for Robert but also that God would give her discernment. He told her to trust her gut. He believed her instincts would open her eyes if she allowed herself to see the truth, assuring her the Holy Spirit would tell her what she could not see for herself.

This was all so new to Faith. On her way home she poured out her heart to her Savior, asking Him to lead and show her the secret sins of her husband—iniquities she had chosen to ignore.

That evening when Robert got home, he was met with a different wife. The always hopeful, always trusting, full-of-tears wife had moved out—a newer version of Faith, who would see what she didn't want to see, had moved in.

"Robert, I went and visited Jack at his office today. I think that you should go speak to him about what is going on in your life."

Robert asked Faith if she had told Jack that someone stole their car.

"No, because it wasn't stolen."

"What do you mean?" Robert asked, exasperated by her apparently brand-new intuition.

"Your car wasn't stolen. I don't know what happened, but I know you're lying to me." She looked him directly in the eye.

Crossing his arms tightly around his torso, Robert stuffed his voice behind his duplicitous heart.

Unstoppable Truth: Shattered

We can all have misconstrued ideas about submission and the role of strength in women of God. I know—that was one of the biggest "frogs in boiling water" lessons that I had to learn. I needed God to remind me of how He had formed me and of the strength He wanted to fill me with. It was life-changing.

Eventually the cock comes home to roost. (Oh, my goodness—I love it when my mother's words spring into my mind.). Eventually our bad choices are going to come back and plant themselves right on our laps. It was true for Haman, Robert, and us.

1. Please read Esther 7:1–10, because this is where the rubber hits the road! (Thanks, Mom!) Yes, Esther is being dramatic. But this is not a waste of hot air; she is unfolding Haman's plot and is going to call him out.

    - Even before Esther makes her request, what does the king promise her (verse 2)?
    - What is Esther's request (verse 3)?
    - Describe the humility and wisdom in her request.
    - Why does she need the king's help (verse 4)?
    - Again, how does she show humility and wisdom (verse 4)?

2. Oh, man! What is the king's reaction (verse 5)?

3. Cock-a-doodle-do! What happens next in Esther 7:6–8?

4. In Esther 7:9–10, how did Haman fall into the very trap he had set for Mordecai? (Warning: don't mess with a God who always has a plan and an obedient woman who has nothing to lose!)

As I consider this scene, I can't help but wonder if Mordecai, standing outside the gate, could have imagined how his beautiful adopted daughter rose to the occasion, risking her position and her very life. What a wonderful example he had been to her!

I love how God works. As the king with insomnia read the annals, he realized he blew it by not honoring the man who had saved his life. God works behind the scenes. When we begin to wonder how we are going to fix the huge problems in our lives, He is at work.

Robert's plan, like Haman's, is unraveling at this point in our story. Robert, like Haman, lost sight of who he was. Pride blinded them. Haman (and the king also) had no idea how the devil was leading them via his evil plot. This is true of Robert as well.

But God had a plan. *But God . . .*

What I really love in this biblical narrative is that Mordecai understood providence. We see it when he says, "Do not think that because you are in the king's house you alone of all the Jews will escape. For if you remain silent at this time, relief and deliverance for the Jews will arise from another place, but you and your father's family will perish. And who knows but that you have come to your royal position for such a time as this?" (Esther 4:13–14 NIV). He may not have had the total picture of how this would come to pass, but he just took one courageous step at a time and expected his (adopted) child to do the same. Esther did not know that God would have a providential plan for her life.

So, child of God, what courageous action is God calling you to take?

Robert's sin took him farther than he ever thought it would. Because Faith trusted in God, she was the person God used to courageously confront him. It would change his life, just as Esther had a part in fulfilling God's grand purpose.

Mordecai exchanged ashen garments for a royal robe. Faith slipped out of a blanket of shame and was soon crowned in righteousness.

Dear reader, God has a courageous calling for you as well. I pray that you would ask Him for wisdom, then step out in faith! He loves you and He's got you!

Chapter 11

Reckoning

"He slept where?" Debbie's muscles tightened as her mouth fell open.

"On the couch." Faith glanced over at her loyal friend on the elliptical machine next to her.

Tawana wiped the sweat from her forehead and chugged half a bottle of water. "Why would you let the man who cheated on you and caused so much heartache sleep on your couch? I wouldn't let him sleep on my *doorway*."

An ocean full of tears hadn't changed a thing. Excuse followed excuse and lie followed lie. The only thing that changed was Faith's insight and strength. Because when a woman of God draws near to Him, that same loving God will whisper sweet words of counsel, giving her unfaltering strength, unspeakable peace, and unfathomable wisdom. And sometimes misunderstood kindness.

Destructive deception had taken Robert and Faith down an unrelenting trajectory toward divorce.

"I think it is important that the kids see their dad." Faith avoided the stares. "And he is having a rough time right now. His job isn't going so well, and even though he is sharing an apartment with a couple of other guys, the prices in Chicago are through the roof."

"He's living in an apartment with other guys? That has to be odd!" Tawana stared with eyes widened at Debbie.

"Yeah, I think it is pretty humbling." Faith raised her eyebrows and shrugged. "That isn't going well either. They are in their twenties and even when Robert was young, that was not his scene."

"It sounds like he has changed a lot in the last few years. Maybe it's his scene now." Debbie shook her head and wiped her arms as she took in a deep breath.

"He's not the same man I fell in love with." Faith's gaze dropped to the ground. "He used to be the most charming, thoughtful, tender guy I had ever met."

"What happened?" Debbie was stumped.

"His success went to his head. He's a self-made man. He worked hard for what he accomplished in business, and I think it eventually destroyed him. And us. He thinks he is his accomplishments." The years had given Faith an understanding of Robert's true motivations. Years and God. After a pause, she looked at her now-thinner self in the mirror. "I think we can all be misled by that. Right?" She smiled at her gym partners.

"But there by the grace of God go I," Debbie conceded, throwing a moist towel in the basket.

"True." Tawana nodded. "But I still can't believe you're letting him sleep there." She shook her head.

"It's good for the kids to see him, and it's good for him to see the kids too." Faith's compassion was genuine. And uncommon. "I've asked my friends to find it in their hearts to be nice to Robert. He's going to church with us on Sunday." Faith wiped down the elliptical she had been using.

"This Sunday? Why?" Tawana's eyes got as big as saucers and darted back and forth at Debbie and Faith.

"Because he is here for Maddison's birthday, and we go to church on Sundays." Faith was firm.

"I think we just want to protect you—that's all." Debbie took a towel from the stack and wiped her brow. "Not very forgiving, are we?" She looked at Tawana.

"I get it. And I appreciate it. I know you love me, but I still love Robert and am praying that God will continue to chase down his stubborn hide." Faith looked them both in the eye and smiled. What would she have done without them over the past five years, the roughest years of her life?

"Has Robert ever spoken to anyone about what he has done? You know, someone like a counselor?" Debbie asked as she grabbed her jacket from her locker.

"Yes, you both remember, right? How we crossed the country going to numerous Christian counselors. He just wasn't honest. He said what they wanted to hear but then returned to his old ways." Faith's heartache was replaced with resolve.

"We'll be nice on Sunday," Debbie conceded.

"And we'll pray." Tawana smiled at Debbie as both pals embraced Faith.

The following Sunday Robert joined Faith for church. "Pretty much describes my life these last few years," Robert whispered as he leaned over to Faith.

"What?" She had been preoccupied with picking up a Lego piece from under the pew that Peter had dropped.

"What he just said." Robert nodded toward the pulpit. "Good understanding gains favor, but the way of the unfaithful is hard."

"Which part?" Faith whispered, glancing into her favorite blue eyes.

"It's been so hard, Faith." His tears were real.

Absorbing a breath bathed in prayer, Faith sat silently, staring forward through the rest of the sermon. She tried to gather her thoughts, begging God for wisdom.

After the kids went to bed that evening, Robert asked if he could stay and talk. He poured out his regret. He owned everything—his cheating, his many indulgences, his not fulfilling his role as a husband and father, and most of all his pride. He saw it all clearly now. The scales had fallen from his eyes and the blinders had been removed.

Faith sat quietly, praying and asking God if it was genuine as he wept inconsolably.

Unstoppable Truth: Reckoning

"For what does it benefit a person to gain the whole world, and forfeit his soul?"
(Mark 8:36)

"God isn't late with his promise as some measure lateness. He is restraining himself on account of you, holding back the End because he doesn't want anyone lost. He's giving everyone space and time to change."
(2 Peter 3:8b-9 MSG)

The words above are exactly what God did in Robert's life. And I gratefully praise Him for doing that in the lives of some of the people I love. He is giving them time to decide! Thank you, Lord Jesus! My prayer is that they will come to Him while they still have time. That is a part of our free will. We have freedom to choose to follow Him or say no to His leading.

"For all have sinned and fall short of the glory of God."
(Romans 3:23)

Our choices always have consequences.

We will all come to a day of reckoning, having to answer for our choices. Like a balance sheet, our decisions will be itemized, our choices and our sins tallied. That is unless we have evaluated and weighed our ownership of those sins and have asked the one who has the power and the means to pay our debt, Christ Jesus, to cover those sins for us.

> *"For the wages of sin is death, but the gift of God is eternal life in Christ Jesus our Lord."*
> (Romans 6:23 NIV)

It is then that our balance sheet will say *paid in full*, written with the crimson ink of Christ's blood.

> *"But when the kindness and love of God our Savior appeared, he saved us, not because of righteous things we had done, but because of his mercy. He saved us through the washing of rebirth and renewal by the Holy Spirit, whom he poured out on us generously through Jesus Christ our Savior, so that, having been justified by his grace, we might become heirs having the hope of eternal life."*
> (Titus 3:4–7 NIV)

If we choose to carry our balance sheet ourselves, thinking we can do so, as Robert did for a time, we will face God on Judgment Day. We will also answer to Him here on earth because He loves us too much to just let us flounder in sin, hurting ourselves and others. The hefty price of sin has a cost. Because of His love for us, He doesn't want us to pay that cost here on earth or for eternity.

If we have trusted Him as our Savior, He whispers words of courage to us to be in step with Him as He makes us new creations (2 Corinthians 5:17; Philippians 1:6). He also guides us through His word and through His Spirit, who abides in us, so our choices will please Him (Proverbs 4:4).

> *"This is how much God loved the world:*
> *He gave his Son, his one and only Son. And this is*
> *why: so that no one need be destroyed; by believing*
> *in him, anyone can have a whole and lasting life.*
> *God didn't go to all the trouble of sending his*
> *Son merely to point an accusing finger, telling the*
> *world how bad it was. He came to help, to put the*
> *world right again. Anyone who trusts in him is*
> *acquitted; anyone who refuses to trust him has*
> *long since been under the death sentence without*
> *knowing it. And why? Because of that person's*
> *failure to believe in the one-of-a-kind Son*
> *of God when introduced to him."*
> (John 3:16–18 MSG)

Haman had choices. Robert had choices. I've had choices. And you have choices.

1. Please read Esther 7:1–5. The plot thickens as Esther stirs up a new plan with the perfect words found in verse 3. Why do you think Esther phrased her response in such a way?

2. Now read Esther 7:6–8. What did Haman do?

3. When caught in a sin, what did Robert do at first?
   - Instead of sincere remorse, what was Haman's reaction (Esther 7:8–10)?
   - What was the tragic outcome of Haman's choices?

We all make decisions. God did not create human robots. He chose to give us free will. Just like Adam and Eve, we choose to do the right thing or to live in disobedience. Not acting on the prompting of God is deciding. All of us know that when we ignore difficult decisions, like health concerns or children's tantrums, we are making a choice. When we procrastinate with even positive opportunities like a wedding invitation, we are choosing to miss a celebration. We know that not acting or not choosing is deciding.

Whenever I have made poor choices, and there have been plenty, I have usually paid a price I did not want to pay. I have also been given boatloads of mercy. As I have learned to listen to God's Spirit at those merciful times, I hear Him gently whisper correction. And I am continually trying to remind myself to listen and thank Him for being such a kind teacher. Both His chastisement *and* His tender whispers are gifts because I am His beloved child.

Choose wisely today, while you still have the choice:

> *"But when the Day of God's Judgment does come, it will be unannounced, like a thief. The sky will collapse with a thunderous bang, everything disintegrating in a raging inferno, earth and all its works exposed to the scrutiny*

> *of Judgment. Since everything here today might well be gone tomorrow, do you see how essential it is to live a holy life? Daily expect the Day of God, eager for its arrival. The galaxies will burn up and the elements melt down that day—but we'll hardly notice. We'll be looking the other way, ready for the promised new heavens and the promised new earth, all landscaped with righteousness."*
> (2 Peter 3:10–13 MSG)

4. Please read Proverbs 22:1. What did Robert come to realize?
   - In Matthew 16:26 what does God want us to acknowledge as we are striving for success?

5. Please read 2 Corinthians 7:8–11. What do true obedience and repentance look like? How does this contrast to what we see in Acts 5:1–10? In your own words, please explain what sincere repentance looks like.

6. As he sat in church, the truths of God's Word spoke to Robert's heart. He had a choice to either stuff them and try to ignore what he was hearing, or he could act in obedience to what the pastor read from the Bible.

   If we give up and turn our backs on all we've learned, all we've been given, all the truth we know, we repudiate Christ's sacrifice and are left on our own to face the Judgment—and a mighty fierce judgment it will be! (Hebrews 10:26–27).

As I noted at the beginning of this book, these storylines are true scenarios of my life as well as people I have known. They are compilations. I want to give you an encouraging update on the couple whom much of the story of Robert and Faith was taken from. More than twenty years later, they are now flourishing.

They sauntered into their first-class seats for an all-expense-paid trip to the Bahamas. Robert's hard work had paid off, and he was at the top of his game with his company. His company had awarded the trip to him. Faith nuzzled beside him as she had for the past sixteen years since their remarriage.

Every day of their four years of divorce had been hard on Robert. Those days had been hard on Faith and their children too. But God did what He does best; He restored the days that the locusts had stolen.

Robert is again successful in business, but most importantly, he is a rockstar in the important areas of life. He and Faith are respected members of their church, offering wisdom and counsel to others who have struggled within their marriage. They both teach others from the Scripture. Most importantly, they are phenomenal examples to their adult children and six beautiful grandchildren.

> *"EVERYONE WHO CALLS ON THE NAME*
> *OF THE LORD WILL BE SAVED."*
> (Romans 10:13)

Reflection: Dear reader, what is the Spirit of God saying to you? If you hear Him speaking, respond in prayer. In the space below write any promptings the Spirit of God may be impressing on your heart.

Setting Your Own Goals

*"He who does not use his endeavors to heal himself
is brother to him who commits suicide."*
(Proverbs 18:9b AMPC)

Faith, Esther, and I rebuilt our lives. All the areas that were on faulty ground impacted each other—our finances affected our emotions, and in my case it prompted me to return to college.

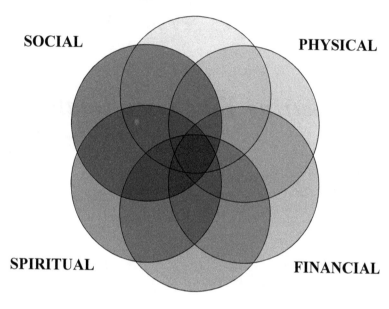

Ultimately, the foundation that we all needed was to be built on a deeper understanding of God and His love and calling for each of us.

The diagram above illustrates all the sectors that needed to change in my life. These are the areas I set goals in with the direction of the master craftsman. Faith sought God to help her also. Because of everything she had been through, she needed to learn to trust Him with her emotions, finances, physical well-being, and understanding of His unconditional love for her.

My heart's desire is to stand beside you as you peer out the window of your life. Imagine that I am taking your hand and putting it in God's. He will help you rebuild, just as He did for me. Hold tightly. He's got this!

As we do in each book in this series, in this chapter we will utilize the acronym CREATE. As we do, create a new story for your life. Because Faith, Esther, and I needed to see God more clearly to be able to change the other areas of our lives, I will share some of the spiritual goals that God led me to embark on.

Trusting God in the Dark

As I leaped from the chair, where comfort mingles with inspiration, I headed toward the kitchen. It was time for some of those delicious sea salt dark chocolate squares my best friend gifted me from New York.

"Who's that?" My chest pounded and my eyes bulged. In the stillness of the twilight, a figure in red was watching me through the window. *Who is that?* My throat held back a gasp. Sleeking into the dark kitchen where those chocolates had beckoned, I peered stealthily from the corner of the window and waited. Slowly I crept closer to get the full view of anyone who might be going down the back stairs. Checking for any movement, my eyes darted back and forth from the steps to the closest place to hide. My nocturnal visitor had vanished. It must have been a young, strong person because he or she moved so swiftly, I reasoned.

What should I do? I grabbed the box of the salted fear-take-awayers. Nibbling those delicious chocolates did dissuade the terror—a little. *Are my eyes playing a trick on me?* As I stared, fixed on that window, I reached into the chocolates, grasping comfort. I swallowed the last morsel, and the tingling in my chest persisted. I slid my hand toward my phone. The small-town police would be right there.

"When did this happen, ma'am?" The officer who looked like a kid who cruises around in the patrol car narrowed his eyes at the glass pane.

"About a half-hour ago. I wasn't sure if I should call." I licked my lips and questioned my eyes.

"Ma'am, I am going to drive around town and look for the person fitting your description. Please call us immediately if this ever happens again."

"Okay, officer. I will." I bolted the door behind him.

On a dark summer evening about six months later, I rose from that same writing chair. Unbuttoning the light sweater I wear in the cool of the evening, I headed toward the kitchen for a glass of water. The figure was back. Right there. In the window. My heart pounding and my mind steady, I halted my swift steps. Slipping my cell phone from my pocket, I crept closer. This time I would be sure to give a better description. I slowed. The figure slowed. I stopped. The figure stopped. As we looked at one another, I saw that the menace was dressed exactly like me. From head to toe.

Are you kidding me? I reprimanded myself. I had been afraid of my own reflection.

This true tale is an illustration of what was going on in my soul for way too long. Fear had seized me and put me in a headlock. I wrestled that beast every day. It usually won. It woke me in the middle of the night. It haunted me at work. It stalked me most days.

But not anymore. Fear does not have a hold of me. I studied its ploys. I gave it to God. I reasoned with my heart, knowing it didn't have control. On most days those actions worked, but at other times they tried to revisit me, threatening to steal my peace.

Then one night the Spirit of God firmly announced, "That is not faith." He was not mincing words. They were kind yet clear. I like it when God talks to me like that.

So, friend, I want to encourage you to ask if you are living in faith at this moment.

You were born to be fearless. You were born to change the world. The night I was afraid of my own reflection was during a time when God was teaching me to live a fearless life. Little by little He was doing His work. As I saw Him working, I also invested in the process.

Author Jerry Bridges puts it this way:

> *Any training—physical, mental, or spiritual—is characterized at first by failure. We fail more often than we succeed. But if we persevere, we gradually see progress till we are succeeding more often than failing. This is true as we seek to put to death particular sins. At first it seems we are making no progress, so we become discouraged and think, What's the use?! I can never overcome that sin. That is exactly what Satan wants us to think. It is at this point that we must exercise perseverance. We keep wanting instant success, but holiness doesn't come that way. Our sinful habits are not broken overnight. Follow-through is required to make any change in our lives, and follow-through requires perseverance.*[1]

---

1. https://gracequotes.org/author-quote/jerry-bridges/page/2/ #108.

As you sit alone with the God who loves you as His beloved bride and as you create your goals, I want to share some thoughts that may be helpful. These are things He spoke to me in our quiet moments. Read and consider each action below and write in your journal what the Spirit of God is whispering to you regarding this action plan.

CREATE your plan.

- **Captivate:** yourself in God's Word and let Him direct, teach, and love you.

- **Realize:** a better way is possible. He has a plan, and it is good.

- **Envision:** dream about what peace could look like and feel like. What is He telling you? Do you need to prioritize reading your Bible? What are your spiritual goals? How will they impact the other goals in your life, especially your emotional goals? How is God directing you and redirecting you?

- **Aim (design and plan):** aim to please Him. Put it into practice. Where, when, and how will you make this change? For example, how do you see your emotions getting in the way of how you want to bring God glory? What actions or reactions are barriers to being who God desires you to be—a woman of dignity and honor? How will you retrain yourself and those around you to make sure you succeed? When will you start? I am praying for you, friend! We will work on this together!

- **Transform:** bring everything you're learning, especially about God's love for you, into your future. He will change the way you think. Yes, spiritually, but also emotionally, and all other areas of your life.
- **Enjoy:** what God is going to do in your life, my amazing, brave friend. Yes, brave. What you are doing takes tremendous courage. You are courageous to be on this journey.

For each of us the spiritual work will be unique because we are each inimitable and each of our lives is unmatched. I encourage you to spend a significant amount of time in the Word and in prayer. Ask God where He wants to take you. He loves you and will lead you gently, just as He has me. Then go there . . . be all in, my dear friend!

How will you get there? And how will you know when you are there? Spiritual goals may not be as measurable as losing twenty pounds but are so much more important. Sometimes we don't even know what God desires to change in us until we ask.

Remember to energize your dreams (don't settle). As you accomplish one dream, celebrate and then energize your next dream. What do you want next?

Your Goals

To find out what you should do, begin praying. The Bible says it this way: "Don't fret or worry. Instead of worrying, pray. Let petitions and praises shape your worries into prayers, letting God know your concerns. Before you know it, a sense of God's wholeness, everything coming together for good, will come and settle you down. It's wonderful what happens when Christ displaces worry at the center of your life" (Philippians 4:6–9 MSG).

Summing it all up, friends, I'd say you'll do best by filling your minds and meditating on things true, noble, reputable, authentic, compelling, gracious—the best, not the worst; the beautiful, not the ugly; things to praise, not things to curse. Put into practice what you learned from this book—what you heard, saw, and realized. Do that and God, who makes everything work together, will work you into His most excellent harmonies.

1. As you prayed about your spiritual goals, what did God show you that He wants you to start doing today to grow spiritually? (Please include today's date.)

2. How do these choices fit the big picture of the life of dignity, passion, and purity that God has for you?

3. What is He nudging you to stop doing today?

The world will give us plenty of reasons to fear. Our flesh, like me when I was scared of my reflection, will give us reasons to fear, and the devil wants us to fear. Because when fear consumes us and becomes an idol, then it has power in our lives. That is how Haman tried to manipulate Mordecai. Only God deserves to be that powerful.

I did everything to overcome my fear; I listened to calming white noise, I took an over-the-counter sleep aid, I prayed constantly, and I memorized scripture. I believe those things were helpful, but the significant cure that caused me to never look back was when I heard the Holy Spirit say, "Fear is not faith. They cannot coincide together."

4. What additional buy-in, cooperation, and encouragement do you need? From whom?

5. How will you keep these in front of you? I have two identical note cards I have written. One is on my mirror so I can see it when get ready in the morning, and the other is in my car. The bullet points of my goals are listed. Writing them down and looking at them every day impacts your success.

My friend, the Holy Spirit will guide you. He promises.

When I was training for my marathon at forty-nine years old on those long country roads, I did a lot of thinking. The mantra the Spirit of God gave me was *Dig deep*. The amazing thing was that it became a mantra for many areas of my life, not just running. At times you will want to give up. During those times, *dig deeper* than you have before. You want to get to the next level. Because in running and in life, improving means challenging where you are now. We need stamina to live this Christ-honoring life.

Merriam-Webster's Dictionary defines *stamina* as "The bodily or mental capacity to sustain a prolonged stressful effort or activity."[2]

---
2. https://www.merriam-webster.com/dictionary/stamina.

Spiritually, God wanted me to challenge my previous thoughts and beliefs. One thing He has taught me is that He can handle it: all my thoughts, fears, and questions. He has all the answers. He is just waiting for me to come to Him with the questions.

Jesus's words in Mark 8 beckon us to what it looks like to be true followers of His. That is where we must begin to change; let Him take over. I love how the message makes it clear as day. Please read the entire chapter and write in your journal what the Spirit of God is telling you!

In the heat of my spiritual growth, God gave me Joshua 1:1–9. I read it every morning for months before even beginning my quiet time. I needed it desperately. I still do. It was my manna. It still is. I want to strongly encourage you to write it on a note card(s) and meditate on it throughout the day.

God has a beautiful plan for each of us. We know His plan for us is good. Jeremiah 29:11–13 (NIV) says it this way: "'For I know the plans I have for you,' declares the Lord, 'plans to prosper you and not to harm you, plans to give you hope and a future. Then you will call on me and come and pray to me, and I will listen to you. You will seek me and find me when you seek me with all your heart.'" These hopeful words in Jeremiah were written to God's people who were in Babylonian exile. These words bolstered their courage that their seventy-year captivity would be met with hope and a future. We see the theme of Jeremiah 29:11–13 throughout the Bible. May we cling to these encouraging truths as well as the admonition given in this passage: call, come and pray, and seek with all of your heart.

Do you see those words? It is His plan. What does He plan? To prosper you and to give you hope and a future. What does he not intend to do? To harm you! What is our responsibility in this plan? Call on Him and seek Him with all our hearts. When we do that, what does He promise is His response? He listens.

Not to harm you. Sometimes in life God says no. I have had my share of those times. Most of them had to do with some hunky guy. It reminds me of the Garth Brooks song "Unanswered Prayers." Oh, how many times I begged God to answer my prayers and made sincere vows of eternal devotion if He did. After nights of endless pleading, why couldn't God see it my way? How could God not answer my prayer? I had it all figured out.

God looked down and said, "No, that would harm you."

I see that now.

God plans that I would live a life of surrender to His will. In those tough times of pleading our prayers, we can trust that He knows and does what is best to bring us peace. Unending and unstoppable peace. His peace.

He tells us what is best. The clearest way God shows us His will is through the Word of God, the Bible. He tells us how He wants us to live. For example, don't have any God other than Him. Don't murder. Don't lust after your neighbor's stuff, including his wife. These are just three of His top ten (Exodus 20:1–17). Why would He say these difficult things? Because He loves us. He knows better than we do the harm that will come into our lives if we do not obey. We also see the harm these sins have caused in our lives or the lives of those around us.

His Word was given to us so we would know Him and so we would become like Jesus.

> *"We have peace with God through our Lord Jesus Christ . . . by faith into this grace in which we stand; and we celebrate in hope of the glory of God. And not only this, but we also celebrate in our tribulations, knowing that tribulation brings about perseverance; and perseverance, proven character; and proven character, hope; and hope does not disappoint, because the love of God has been poured out within our hearts through the Holy Spirit who was given to us."*
> (Romans 5:1–5)

Why would we celebrate in our tribulations, as when God says no? It reminds me of what James says when he tells us to consider it joy, actually *pure joy*, when we face trials (James 1:2). Jesus and Stephen faced fatal trials, and both uttered the similar words "Forgive them" (Luke 23:34; Acts 7:60). The great ones had this attitude in common, including the mother of Jesus, who when she was expecting and faced an uncertain future, said, "I am the Lord's servant . . . May your word to me be fulfilled" (Luke 1:38 NIV).

There was a time for my heartbreak. There was a time to dig—I mean to dig deeper than I have ever dug into God's Word and to listen to God's still, small voice. Then there was a time to change and grow. Now it's your turn.

A personal reflection: Littering my writing space are the journals, thousands of note cards, books I devoured, and the tear-stained scraps of paper from the hardest days of my life. Are they like a dream now? No, they are something altogether different. They are like when I trained for a marathon at the age of forty-nine, times ten. They represent the time when I didn't think I could carry myself another day, so I let God carry me.

Ask God for clarity. Friend, as I expressed before, in the landscape of decisions are hidden landmines called rotten, hurtful choices. Buried deep beneath the overgrowth hides the quicksand where people sometimes look for answers. These are well-timed and strategically hidden traps. They are prepared by the devil and his minions who live alongside us. They are also promoted by the world and your fleshly desires (Ephesians 2:1–3).

- **Romantic relationships:** relationships to fill a void are not the same as waiting for the God-honoring relationship that God may be preparing for you

- **Status:** consider if you are seeking a position to feel important instead of to honor God

- **Kids:** an unhealthy reliance on your children, including adult children

- **Friends:** trusting the opinions of friends more than depending on God

- **Unhealthy living:** smoking, drinking, and drugs

- **Retaliation:** wanting to get even or to prove a point to the person or people who hurt you

After my marriage shattered, I became attracted to someone else. I am so grateful that God was still my main person because He gave me the greatest gift I needed at the time: clarity. I never dishonored myself or God. The attraction never blossomed into a relationship. That was God.

The clarity that God provided was seeing some of my old patterns of unhealthy thinking that were trying to invade my newly shaped heart. I knew I was capable of stacking crumbling bricks onto something that was bound to fail. I cried out to God for insight.

Friends, I don't hear God's voice audibly, but sometimes I hear it so clearly in my heart that it might as well be on a loudspeaker at a football field.

As I stepped over the railroad tracks, deep in prayer . . . Okay, actually if I remember it correctly, I was telling God my plan about how this could all work out just perfectly. My inner dialogue rambled.

He'll do this. Then I'll say this. Then He will make this commitment. Then you, God, you will do this.

"Girl, you don't want that." His Spirit stopped me in my tracks.

When I realized with the help of the Holy Spirit what I was doing, I began dismantling the façade I was producing in my emotions. The blessing of insight I had been given was in realizing it was my problem. Because it was mine and mine alone. With God's help I could change it.

I asked myself if the basics of a relationship—caring, honesty, and respect—were there in this friendship. They were not. Hard truth. This was a romanticized dream. Call it what it is . . . God gave me the wisdom to take the shackles off the other person I was attracted to and walk away.

The crazy thing is, after I emotionally walked away, I realized he missed the attention I was showering on him. (Beware, friends, if you are in the same scenario). Be strong and stay away!

Now, my beautiful new friend, I want to encourage you to dig deep into your own goals. Utilize the CREATE acronym for all the areas in which God is speaking to you. But be sure to move forward in your new life. Press on and allow God to change everything that needs to change. He is for you and so am I. Be loved!

ADDENDUM

The following areas help us live out our faith, to know how to grow in tribulations. They are the daily disciplines that God will use to transform us if we will surrender to Him and His ways.

- **God's Word:** God urges us to read and meditate on His Word all day, and all night and to live what we read so we can be prosperous and successful (Joshua 1:8 NASB). We are told that Scripture was breathed from God's mouth to teach, to rebuke, to correct, and to train us to a righteous life so that we are prepared to do any good work (2 Timothy 3:16–17 ESV).

- **Memorization:** One of the ways we can grow spiritually is by memorizing the scripture that God prompts in our hearts. We read in the Bible that this will help us obey God and not sin against Him (Psalm 119:11 CEB). This is one of the most life-changing action points God has used to transform me. I have thousands of cards from instances when He prompted me over the years. They are taped to my bathroom mirror, and they are in my car, purse, and kitchen counter. I have carried them on long walks and to work. I have taken pictures of them with my phone and given them away. They are hidden everywhere so His Word can be hidden in my heart.

- **Church membership:** There are many reasons the Bible tells us it is so important to not stop meeting together (Hebrews 10:24–25 NASB). A great picture of what a church family should look like is in the book of Acts. "They devoted themselves to the apostles' teaching and to fellowship, to the breaking of bread and to prayer. Everyone was filled with awe at the many wonders and signs performed by the apostles. All the believers were together and had everything in common. They sold property and possessions to give to anyone who had need. Every day they continued to meet together in the temple courts. They broke bread in their homes and ate together with glad and sincere hearts, praising God and enjoying the favor of all the people. And the Lord added to their number daily those who were being saved" (Acts 2:42–47 NIV).

- **Service:** Whenever I get too caught up in my to-do list, I open the Bible and turn to Philippians 2. It straightens out any thoughts of entitlement I may be considering, and that is exactly what I need sometimes. Because Jesus, the one I am striving to be like, shows me what service—His type of service—looks like.

> *"Is there any encouragement from belonging to Christ? Any comfort from his love? Any fellowship together in the Spirit? Are your hearts tender and compassionate? Then make me truly happy by agreeing wholeheartedly with each other, loving one another, and working together with one mind and*

purpose. Don't be selfish; don't try to impress others. Be humble, thinking of others as better than yourselves. Don't look out only for your own interests, but take an interest in others, too. You must have the same attitude that Christ Jesus had. Though he was God, he did not think of equality with God as something to cling to. Instead, he gave up his divine privileges; he took the humble position of a slave and was born as a human being. When he appeared in human form, he humbled himself in obedience to God and died a criminal's death on a cross."
(Philippians 2:1–7 NLT)

- **Tithing and giving to the poor:** I am so grateful that at a young age, just after I started walking with Christ, I learned about tithing. It has been a discipline that has brought me immense peace. Why? Because, I learned the truth—that everything I have, including my abilities to earn a living, come from God. He gave me my gifts, talents, and even provided for my training (Psalm 24:1–6 NLT). Because of His provision, He desires that I give back just a portion of what is His.

"Honor the Lord with your wealth and with the best part of everything you produce. Then he will fill your barns with grain, and your vats will overflow with good wine."
(Proverbs 3:9–10 NLT)

God has taught me two important aspects regarding tithing.

Number one, I am to give to Him first. Not only does the Bible note that is how it should be done, but I know if I wait until I start paying for other needs, it won't happen. Since I was babysitting as a preteen, I have been slipping part of what belongs to Him right in my Bible so I will be sure to do first things first.

Number two, I learned that because I'm giving a significant amount of money, I need to choose my church family and other organizations carefully. I try to do my due diligence so I can know I am giving to communities that are striving to serve God and His purposes.

- **Healthy friendships:** Godly, loyal, honest friends are some of the greatest gifts we can have. On my good days, as we love and celebrate one another, the sun is bright, the clouds are loftier, and my heart sings in tune. On crummy days I am not alone. I am held and I am encouraged by them to keep going. In the following scripture we see that is exactly what God had in mind. I am blessed with the true friends God has given me.

> *"I observed yet another example of something meaningless under the sun. This is the case of a man who is all alone, without a child or a brother, yet who works hard to gain as much wealth as he can. But then he asks himself, "Who am I working for? Why am I giving up so much pleasure now?" It is all so*

meaningless and depressing. Two people are better off than one, for they can help each other succeed. If one person falls, the other can reach out and help. But someone who falls alone is in real trouble. Likewise, two people lying close together can keep each other warm. But how can one be warm alone? A person standing alone can be attacked and defeated, but two can stand back-to-back and conquer. Three are even better, for a triple-braided cord is not easily broken.

(Ecclesiastes 4:7–12 NLT)

GLOSSARY

Bully: "Bullying is a distinctive pattern of repeatedly and deliberately harming and humiliating others, specifically those who are smaller, weaker, younger, or in any way more vulnerable than the bully. The deliberate targeting of those of lesser power is what distinguishes bullying from garden-variety aggression. Bullying can involve verbal attacks (name-calling and making fun of others) as well as physical ones, threats of harm, other forms of intimidation . . ."[1]

Codependency: "Codependency is a dysfunctional relationship dynamic where one person assumes the role of 'the giver,' sacrificing their own needs and well-being for the sake of the other, 'the taker.' The bond in question doesn't have to be romantic; it can occur just as easily between parent and child, friends, and family members."[2]

Gaslighting: "an elaborate and insidious technique of deception and psychological manipulation, usually practiced by a single deceiver, or 'gaslighter,' on a single victim over an extended period. Its effect is to gradually undermine the victim's confidence in his ability to distinguish truth from falsehood, right from wrong, or reality from appearance, thereby rendering

---
1. https://www.psychologytoday.com/us/basics/bullying.
2. https://www.psychologytoday.com/intl/basics/codependency.

him pathologically dependent on the gaslighter in his thinking or feelings."[3]

Groupthink: "Groupthink is a phenomenon that occurs when a group of well-intentioned people makes irrational or non-optimal decisions spurred by the urge to conform or the belief that dissent is impossible."[4]

Narcissism: "Narcissism is characterized by a grandiose sense of self-importance, a lack of empathy for others, a need for excessive admiration, and the belief that one is unique and deserving of special treatment."[5]

Psychopath: "Antisocial personality disorder, sometimes called sociopathy, is a mental disorder in which a person consistently shows no regard for right and wrong and ignores the rights and feelings of others. People with antisocial personality disorder tend to antagonize, manipulate, or treat others harshly or with callous indifference. They show no guilt or remorse for their behavior."[6]

Trauma bond: "Trauma-bonding is a hormonal attachment created by repeated abuse, sprinkled with being 'saved' every now and then...This type of conditioning is intuitively exploited by narcissists...In conjunction with gaslighting, emotional abuse and manipulation designed to make us question our reality, the major building blocks for trauma-bonding are formed."[7]

---

3. https://www.britannica.com/topic/gaslighting.
4. https://www.psychologytoday.com/us/basics/groupthink
5. https://www.psychologytoday.com/us/basics/narcissism
6. https://www.mayoclinic.org/diseases-conditions/antisocial-personality-disorder/symptoms-causes/syc-2035392
7. https://www.psychologytoday.com/us/blog/emotional-sobriety/202109/what-is-trauma-bonding

Stockholm syndrome: "Stockholm syndrome is a psychological response to being held captive. People with Stockholm syndrome form a psychological connection with their captors and begin sympathizing with them. In addition to the original kidnapper-hostage situation, Stockholm syndrome now includes other types of trauma in which there's a bond between the abuser and the person being abused."[8]

[8.] https://my.clevelandclinic.org/health/diseases/22387-stockholm-syndrome

Printed in the USA
CPSIA information can be obtained
at www.ICGtesting.com
CBHW071045191223
2560CB00005B/19